P9-DIY-519

THE IMPORTANCE OF

William Shakespeare

These and other titles are included in The Importance Of biography series:

Alexander the Great	Harry Houdini
Muhammad Ali	Thomas Jefferson
Louis Armstrong	Mother Jones
James Baldwin	Chief Joseph
Clara Barton	John F. Kennedy
The Beatles	Martin Luther King Jr.
Napoleon Bonaparte	Joe Louis
Julius Caesar	Malcolm X
Rachel Carson	Thurgood Marshall
Charlie Chaplin	Margaret Mead
Charlemagne	Golda Meir
Cesar Chavez	Michelangelo
Winston Churchill	Wolfgang Amadeus Mozart
Cleopatra	John Muir
Christopher Columbus	Sir Isaac Newton
Hernando Cortes	Richard M. Nixon
Marie Curie	Georgia O'Keeffe
Charles Dickens	Louis Pasteur
Emily Dickinson	Pablo Picasso
Amelia Earhart	Elvis Presley
Thomas Edison	Jackie Robinson
Albert Einstein	Norman Rockwell
Duke Ellington	Eleanor Roosevelt
Dian Fossey	Anwar Sadat
Anne Frank	Margaret Sanger
Benjamin Franklin	Oskar Schindler
Galileo Galilei	William Shakespeare
Emma Goldman	John Steinbeck
Jane Goodall	Tecumseh
Martha Graham	Jim Thorpe
Lorraine Hansberry	Mark Twain
Stephen Hawking	Queen Victoria
Ernest Hemingway	Pancho Villa
Jim Henson	H. G. Wells
Adolf Hitler	

THE IMPORTANCE OF

William Shakespeare

by
Thomas Thrasher

Lucent Books, P.O. Box 289011, San Diego, CA 92198-9011

Library of Congress Cataloging-in-Publication Data

Thrasher, Thomas, 1968–
    The importance of William Shakespeare / by Thomas
    Thrasher.
        p.   cm. — (The importance of)
    Includes bibliographical references and index.
    Summary: Discusses the early life, London years, work,
influence, and importance of William Shakespeare.
    ISBN 1-56006-374-2 (lib. bdg. : alk. paper)
    1. Shakespeare, William, 1564–1616—Biography—Juvenile
literature.   2. Dramatists, English—Early modern, 1500–1700—
Biography—Juvenile literature.   [1. Shakespeare, William, 1564–
1616.   2. Authors, English.]   I. Title.   II. Series.
    PR2895.T48   1999
    822.3'3—dc21   98–23166
    [b]   CIP
                                                                   AC

Copyright 1999 by Lucent Books, Inc., P.O. Box 289011,
San Diego, California, 92198-9011

Printed in the U.S.A.

Contents

Foreword

THE IMPORTANCE OF biography series deals with individuals who have made a unique contribution to history. The editors of the series have deliberately chosen to cast a wide net and include people from all fields of endeavor. Individuals from politics, music, art, literature, philosophy, science, sports, and religion are all represented. In addition, the editors did not restrict the series to individuals whose accomplishments have helped change the course of history. Of necessity, this criterion would have eliminated many whose contribution was great, though limited. Charles Darwin, for example, was responsible for radically altering the scientific view of the natural history of the world. His achievements continue to impact the study of science today. Others, such as Chief Joseph of the Nez Percé, played a pivotal role in the history of their own people. While Joseph's influence does not extend much beyond the Nez Percé, his nonviolent resistance to white expansion and his continuing role in protecting his tribe and his homeland remain an inspiration to all.

These biographies are more than factual chronicles. Each volume attempts to emphasize an individual's contributions both in his or her own time and for posterity. For example, the voyages of Christopher Columbus opened the way to European colonization of the New World. Unquestionably, his encounter with the New World brought monumental changes to both Europe and the Americas in his day. Today, however, the broader impact of Columbus's voyages is being critically scrutinized. *Christopher Columbus,* as well as every biography in The Importance Of series, includes and evaluates the most recent scholarship available on each subject.

Each author includes a wide variety of primary and secondary source quotations to document and substantiate his or her work. All quotes are footnoted to show readers exactly how and where biographers derive their information, as well as provide stepping-stones to further research. These quotations enliven the text by giving readers eyewitness views of the life and times of each individual covered in The Importance Of series.

Finally, each volume is enhanced by photographs, bibliographies, chronologies, and comprehensive indexes. For both the casual reader and the student engaged in research, The Importance Of biographies will be a fascinating adventure into the lives of people who have helped shape humanity's past and present, and who will continue to shape its future.

IMPORTANT DATES IN THE LIFE OF WILLIAM SHAKESPEARE

1564
William Shakespeare is born to John and Mary Shakespeare in Stratford-upon-Avon on April 23.

1577
William is withdrawn from school.

1582
William Shakespeare, age eighteen, marries Anne Hathaway, age twenty-six.

1583
Susanna, Shakespeare's first child, is born and baptized on May 26.

1585
Hamnet and Judith, Shakespeare's twin son and daughter are born; Shakespeare leaves Stratford for unknown reasons.

1589
Shakespeare's first play, *Henry VI Part 1,* is performed.

1593
"Venus and Adonis" is written.

1594
"The Rape of Lucrece" is written.

1595
Shakespeare becomes associated with the Lord Chamberlain's Men.

1596
The Shakespeare family is granted a coat of arms; Hamnet, Shakespeare's only son, dies and is buried on August 11.

1597
William Shakespeare purchases New Place in Stratford.

1601
William's father dies; the Lord Chamberlain's Men are investigated for their role in Essex's failed rebellion.

1602
William Shakespeare buys land and homes in Stratford.

1603
Queen Elizabeth dies; King James of Scotland becomes the new ruler of England; after James assumes the throne, the Lord Chamberlain's Men are issued a royal license and change their name to the King's Men in honor of their new patron.

1607
Susanna, Shakespeare's oldest daughter, marries Dr. John Hall on June 5; Shakespeare's youngest brother, Edmund, dies in London and is buried on December 31.

1608
Elizabeth Hall, Shakespeare's first granddaughter, is born and baptized on February 21; Shakespeare's mother, Mary, dies.

1609
Unauthorized publication of Shakespeare's *Sonnets.*

1610
Shakespeare returns to Stratford and begins semiretirement.

1611
Shakespeare writes *The Tempest.*

1613
Shakespeare's only surviving brother, Richard, dies.

1616
Shakespeare's youngest daughter, Judith, marries Thomas Quiney; Shakespeare becomes ill with an unknown sickness and dies.

1623
A monument to Shakespeare is established in the Holy Trinity Church of Stratford; Shakespeare's wife, Anne, dies; the First Folio is published.

Shakespeare as Renaissance Man

Shakespeare is one of those historical figures whose name carries the connotation of genius. His name is mentioned with the same reverence given to those masters of the arts who have become larger than life, so famous that they are known by last names only: Chaucer, Beethoven, Bach, Degas, Monet, Mozart, Picasso. Shakespeare's plays have become such an ingrained part of English-speaking culture that it is impossible to list all his contributions to language, literature, and drama. Although Shakespeare's name and contribution to literature remain awe-inspiring, the man himself was undistinguished.

It is doubtful that William Shakespeare foresaw his future fame. While he lived, he wanted what many people desire: a home in the country, good marriages for his children, and a comfortable retirement for himself. To achieve these things, he worked in the theater as a "bookkeeper," wrote plays, and invested in property. But this is all we know, and even this is partly conjecture. Shakespeare's life is well documented; however, the documentation is more numerous than interesting: receipts, deeds, and various legal documents. Since none of Shakespeare's personal letters or diaries survive, it is impossible to do more than guess at what the man himself was like.

Shakespeare's plays have continued to sell tickets for more than three centuries and show no sign of losing their popularity. William Shakespeare changed the face of English drama from the stiff formalism of the Greco-Roman tradition to something more realistic. His plays are remarkably

William Shakespeare's plays remain the most read and most performed works of all time.

more dynamic than the medieval morality plays he saw as a child and more sophisticated than many of the plays written by his contemporaries.

Shakespeare is both a product of Renaissance England and an embodiment of it. The Elizabethan era was marked by a slight loosening of the rigid class structure that marked the medieval period. More people were leaving the country for the cities; the cities, in turn, were booming with trade from England's colonial holdings; and the merchants and the middle class were getting rich, and beginning to demand a voice in government. The middle class was starting to use its newfound wealth to buy titles and estates in an attempt to join the aristocracy. If it had not been for the expanding middle class and its appetite for entertainment, Shakespeare never would have succeeded. William Shakespeare, born into the working class, managed to work his way into the ranks of the minor gentry through both his artistic and financial success in the relatively new, and secular, realm of the public theater. Shakespeare typifies the Renaissance man: one foot in the past, one foot in the future, and both hands on the present.

1 Shakespeare's Early Life

William Shakespeare's father, John, was a man of humble origins. The son of a tenant farmer from the village of Snitterfield, he left home to take up an apprenticeship as a glove maker in the nearby town of Stratford-upon-Avon. Little did John Shakespeare know that this action would forever link his surname with that of Stratford as the birthplace of the greatest writer in the English language.

Stratford-upon-Avon, located in the county of Warwickshire, nestles against the Avon River at a point where the road from London crosses a bridge on its way to Shrewsbury. It was a town with a bustling marketplace and a proud citizenry. Because of its location on the river, and being the main thoroughfare to London, Stratford attracted farmers from the surrounding countryside who brought their produce and livestock on market days, while local merchants and craftsmen would sell various goods. It was a place where money could be made, and this is why young John Shakespeare came.

When John first arrived in Stratford, he probably worked as an apprentice to a glove maker. After finishing his apprenticeship (a term of about seven years), John established his own shop in Stratford. He began to make gloves and leather goods for the local gentry. He must have

England Today

done well because there are records of him purchasing land and houses in the surrounding area. As a matter of fact, John Shakespeare first appears in local records on April 29, 1552. He was fined for keeping a dunghill on a corner of his newly acquired property on Henley Street.

In 1553, Stratford received its Charter of Incorporation from the Crown. The town could now make its own bylaws and elect a common council of burgesses and aldermen to manage local affairs. John Shakespeare, in addition to running his business, became involved in local politics. In September 1556, he was elected ale-taster, a duty that included making sure that bakers made full-weight loaves of bread and that brewers made untainted ale and beer. Two years later, in 1558, Shakespeare was named a constable (a type of police officer) and it became his job to preserve the peace of the town. In 1559 he was made an affeeror, a person who decided how much to charge for fines. Other promotions followed: From 1561 to 1563 John served as a burgess; in 1565 he was elected an alderman; and in 1568 he was chosen to be the bailiff (a position equivalent to a modern mayor). Eventually, John applied to the College of Arms for a coat of arms, but the request was not granted until 1596. During the English Renaissance, a coat of arms denoted that a family was respectable, established, and a member of the noble class. John Shakespeare had obtained a position of respect in Stratford, a man who came into town as a poor apprentice and managed to establish himself as one of its business and civic leaders.

John Shakespeare married Mary Arden sometime between 1556 and 1558. For John Shakespeare, the marriage would increase his wealth and add a hint of nobility to his otherwise common status. (The Ardens were members of the landed gentry in Warwickshire.) There was also the added satisfaction of marrying the daughter of his father's landlord.

The Ardens, despite a noble heritage, were ordinary folk composed of prosperous farmers and merchants. Mary was the youngest daughter of Robert Arden, and shortly before marrying John, she had inherited a good portion of her father's estate. By marrying John Shakespeare, Mary would receive a degree of status (John was, after all, a successful merchant and a rising local leader) and a husband who could manage her considerable holdings and provide for their growing family.

Youth and Education

In his plays, William Shakespeare displays an intimate knowledge not only of Protestantism but Catholicism. This has caused some scholars to speculate upon the religious beliefs of his parents. During this period of English history, after Henry VIII had broken off ties with the Roman Catholic Church, there was a great deal of anti-Catholic feeling among the people. This anti-Catholic feeling had been amplified by the short reign of Mary Tudor ("Bloody" Mary to her enemies), who had burned Protestants at the stake for their beliefs. When Bloody Mary's younger sister, Elizabeth, who was Protestant, took over, the tables were turned. Protestantism became acceptable, and Catholics who did not change faiths (they were called "recusants") were persecuted. Over William Shakespeare's lifetime there were several attempts by Catholic groups to overthrow the government of Queen Elizabeth (and later James I) and reestablish the Catholic faith as the standard religion of England.

Mary Arden's family was suspected of hiding priests (an offense punishable by death), and John Shakespeare's "Spiritual Last Will and Testament" seems to prove his belief in Catholicism. However, it was during John's time as a burgess that the Stratford council moved to "Protestantize" the Gild Chapel, which meant whitewashing over its Catholic frescoes. It is hard to tell which religion the couple, and for that matter the town, believed in. It could be that John and Mary Shakespeare were law-abiding, churchgoing Protestants during the day and practicing Catholics at night, a

Social Classes in Elizabethan England

In Renaissance England, the social class to which you belonged dictated whom you would marry, whom you would associate with, and how you would earn your living. In the following passage from Shakespeare and Elizabethan Culture, *anthropologist Philip K. Bock examines the various classes:*

"Queen Elizabeth stood at the pinnacle of an aristocracy that was clearly ranked and that was based upon the ideology linking virtue and authority with noble birth. Below the princes of the royal house . . . were the dukes, marquis, and earls who controlled vast land holdings. Next came the viscounts and the more numerous but less powerful barons. Below them were many minor nobles, some only recently elevated to gentility or knighthood. Birth into the higher ranks of nobility insured wealth and privilege. A titled noble could be tried only by his peers (equals in rank), and royalty answered to no one but God. In a court of law the 'word of a gentleman' was accepted without further oath.

Perhaps the most important socioeconomic change of the Elizabethan era was the rise in numbers and power of an urban middle class that ranked between the titled nobility and the rural commoners. Starting during the time of Henry VII, this middle group was recruited from above and below: it included younger sons of noble families who, due to the rule of primogeniture [inheritance], could inherit neither titles nor estates, but was made up primarily of farmers, traders, and professionals who had risen from humble origins to positions of wealth and authority. Their aspirations to 'gentle' status were frequently mocked by the established nobility, but it was soon recognized that new money was as effective as old family in making a gentleman. Prosperous merchants quickly acquired status by purchasing estates and titles for themselves, and education or titled spouses for their offspring."

Queen Elizabeth of England ruled the country through most of Shakespeare's life. Religious controversies prevailed during her reign, and the theater was sometimes affected by these affairs.

situation that would not be unusual for the time. In any case, it is likely that their son William was exposed to the beliefs of both religions.

The Shakespeares were a fruitful couple. Mary gave birth to their first daughter, Joan, in 1558. It is unclear what became of this child, but it is thought that she died while still a baby. Their next child, Margaret, was born in 1562 and died one year later. In 1564, William was born. Two years later, William's younger brother Gilbert was born. Gilbert remained in the Stratford area, became a haberdasher (a merchant who sells buttons, ribbons, and needles), and died in his forty-fifth year. In 1569, William's younger sister Joan was born. She married a hatter by the name of William Hart, had four children, and remained in the Stratford area until her death in 1646. Little is known about the next two Shakespeare children. Anne was born in 1571 and died eight years later.

Richard was born in 1574 and died in 1613. The only thing known about Richard, other than his dates of birth and death, is that he was summoned before the Stratford ecclesiastical (religious) court for an unspecified offense and fined a shilling. William's youngest brother, Edmund, was born in 1580. When he was old enough, he followed his older brother to London and became an actor. It is unknown which acting company Edmund worked with, but he fathered an illegitimate child (who died). A few months after his child died, Edmund expired as well. He was buried in the churchyard of St. Mary Overy in 1607 at the age of twenty-seven.

The exact date of William Shakespeare's birth is unknown. It is known that he was baptized on April 26, 1564. Tradition holds that he was born on April 23, a reasonable assumption because it was customary for parents to christen their child three days after the birth. Whatever the exact date of William's birth, one thing is clear: He survived his infancy (remarkable considering that the bubonic plague visited Stratford the following summer, killing about one-sixth of the entire population).

During the Renaissance, education was a luxury that could only be afforded by the wealthy. Neither John nor Mary Shakespeare could write. This is usual. During Queen Elizabeth's reign, 70 percent of men and 90 percent of women from all classes could not sign their names. However, John and Mary made sure that their son William could not only read, but could write his name as well.

In Stratford, education was free to the sons of its burgesses (the town's representatives to Parliament) and aldermen (similar to councilmen). Women, except in the best of homes, received little education. Male students began to attend classes at the age of five, going first to a "petty" school taught by an abecedarius, or usher. These ushers taught their pupils the alphabet and the Lord's Prayer using a horn book: a piece of paper framed in wood and covered for protection by a thin layer of transparent horn. The mark of the cross preceded the alphabet, so it was called the "Christ cross-row." William Shakespeare was no doubt remembering his horn book when he wrote in *Richard III*, "He hearkens after prophecies and dreams, / And from the cross-row plucks the letter G."[1] At seven years of age, after learning the basics in petty school, the students were ready for grammar school.

Shakespeare was born in the town of Stratford, England (pictured). He received his early education at a "petty" school there.

Based upon comments scattered throughout his plays, Shakespeare may not have enjoyed his school years. In *Romeo and Juliet,* he writes, "Love goes toward love as schoolboys from their books, / But love from love, toward school with heavy looks."[2] Gremio, in *The Taming of the Shrew,* returns from Petruchio's troublesome

The Average School Day

In this excerpt from Young Shakespeare, *Russell Fraser describes the rigorous schedule that Shakespeare would have maintained as a schoolboy during the English Renaissance.*

"Shakespeare with satchel and shining morning face ascended [to the grammar school] by a stone staircase, open to the weather and covered with tile. In the big room at the top of the stairs, haloed saints, much diminished, looked backward to the Middle Ages on the plastered south wall between the studs. Carved bosses in the middle of the roof tied the chamfered [beveled] oak beams together, and painted roses and hearts taught a lesson, political. The red rose of Lancaster showed a white heart. Conciliating differences, the heart of the white Yorkist rose was red. Boys froze in this schoolroom, bitter cold like most public rooms in England. At the head of the room sat the master, enthroned, at the other end his assistant.

He [Shakespeare] started off in 'petty school,' prescribed by statute and lasting two years. The 'petits' . . . sat down with the older boys, doing different things. Summers, school began at 6 A.M., an hour later in winter. It ended at dusk. Boys [no girls were allowed to attend public schools] recited on an empty stomach, not breaking fast till mid-morning. In the afternoon, they had playtime, fifteen minutes for this. They wrestled, leaped, ran, or practiced shooting the longbow, but frivolous sports like bowling were out. Fortune smiling, they got a day off, called a 'remedy.' Masters discouraged this, saying that 'Many remedies make ignorant scholars.' Thursdays and Saturdays, school recessed at noon. Sunday was free. Twelve months of the year, though, no day was wholly free, and boys went to church on free days, supervised by the master. After church he quizzed them, wanting to know about the sermon."

Shakespeare began his rigorous education in a small school such as this one. Many of today's English schools are similar to those of Shakespeare's time.

wedding "As willingly as e'er I came from school."[3] In *2 Henry VI,* the rebel Jack Cade condemns Lord Say to death because

> Thou hast most traitorously corrupted the youth of the realm in erecting a grammar school; and whereas, before, our forefathers had no other books but the score and the tally, thou hast caus'd printing to be us'd. . . . It will be prov'd to thy face that thou hast men about thee that usually talk of a noun and a verb, and such abominable words as no Christian ear can endure to hear. . . . Thou hast put . . . in prison [men], because they could not read, thou hast hang'd them, when, indeed, only for that cause they had been most worthy to live. . . . Away with him, away with him! He speaks Latin.[4]

Regardless of how Shakespeare felt about his schooling, it provided him the "small Latin and less Greek"[5] that he would need to succeed in his chosen profession. In grammar school he studied William Lily's *Short Introduction of Grammar.* The first half of the book laid out the basics of English grammar while the second part contained the rules for Latin. For moral instruction the students would read, in Latin, Erasmus's *Cato,* the fables of Aesop, the *Metamorphoses* of Ovid, and Plutarch's *Lives.* The course of study also included Greco-Roman playwrights (which introduced young William to classical comedy and the five-act structure of plays), rhetoric (which he used for dramatic effect), logic, and numeration.

About 1577, John Shakespeare's fortunes began to decline. In 1578, he mortgaged a house and fifty-six acres (part of his wife's inheritance) to his brother-in-law Lambert Arden for cash. John was unable to repay the loan, and this part of his wife's inheritance was forever lost. Later that same year he mortgaged another section of Mary's inheritance, some eighty-six acres, for a set term of years. John's financial troubles continued. Over the next few years, he had several fines levied against him by the courts for debt. It got so bad

How Educated Was Shakespeare?

A major criticism of William Shakespeare has been that he lacked the education necessary to write the plays. In the following quotation taken from Edmund Chambers's A Short Life of Shakespeare with the Sources, *Shakespeare's first biographer, Nicholas Rowe, speculates upon the extent of Shakespeare's education:*

"His Father, who was a considerable Dealer in Wool, had so large a Family, ten Children in all, that tho' he was his eldest Son, he could give him no better Education than his own Employment. He had bred him, 'tis true, for some time at a Free-School, where 'tis probable he acquir'd that little Latin he was Master of: But the narrowness of his Circumstances, and the want of his assistance at Home, forc'd his Father to withdraw him from thence, and unhappily prevented his further Proficiency in that Language. It is without Controversie, that he had no knowledge of the Writings of the Antient [sic] Poets . . . [and] Whether his Ignorance of the Antients were a disadvantage to him or no, may admit of a Dispute: For tho' the knowledge of 'em might have made him more Correct, yet it is not improbable but that the Regularity and Deference for them, which would have attended that Correctness, might have restrain'd some of that Fire, Impetuosity, and even beautiful Extravagance which we admire in Shakespear: And I believe we are better pleas'd with those Thoughts, altogether New and Uncommon, which his own imagination supply'd him so abundantly. . . . Whatever Latin he had, 'tis certain he understood French, as may be observ'd from many Words and Sentences scatter'd up and down his Plays in that Language."

that the one-time alderman could not appear in church "for feare of process for debtte."[6]

William was directly affected by his father's misfortunes. At thirteen years of age, his father withdrew him from grammar school. Nicholas Rowe, one of Shakespeare's earliest biographers, writes that the narrowness of his father's "circumstances, and the want of his [William's] assistance at home, . . . forc'd his father to withdraw him from thence."[7] One of the biggest debates among Shakespeare scholars is about whether he had enough education to write the plays. Although no firm conclusion can be drawn about this, it must be pointed out that he did have a basic education (math, grammar, reading, writing, and Latin). It is conceivable that Shakespeare continued to educate himself after leaving school, a task made easier because of a burgeoning new business called printing.

At this point in his life, some researchers speculate that William made a connection with a noble family: Through the influence of his mother, he was placed in the home of one of her noble relations as a servant, and there was exposed to higher learning, and the society of the aristocracy. The reason scholars believe this is because his plays demonstrate an advanced education and a knowledge of court life. As plausible as this scenario may be, considering the circumstances of his father, it is more likely that he worked in his father's shop as a glover's apprentice.

In 1582, the glover's apprentice, William Shakespeare, married Anne Hathaway. Like his father, William married a woman of modest social rank. Anne Hathaway was descended from a family of established yeomen (small farmers who cultivate their own land) and had inherited a good sum of money from her father after his death. The Shakespeares and the Hathaways had known each other for years: When William was two years old, his father had stood surety (promised to pay) for two debts that Anne's father, Richard, had accumulated.

Marriage and the "Lost Years"

Anne was eight years older than her husband (she was twenty-six and he was eighteen when they married). Shakespeare had not yet achieved his majority (the age at which a boy legally became a man) and was still considered a minor. Because of his status as a minor, and since the wedding could not be completed before Advent (a religious season during which marriages were normally forbidden), a special license had to be secured from the bishop of Worcester. Once this license had been issued on November 27, 1582, William Shakespeare and Anne Hathaway became man and wife and, according to the custom of the time, moved into his father's house on Henley Street.

Six months later it became obvious why the odd marriage had taken place. Anne gave birth to a daughter, Susanna, on May 26, 1583. Anne must have been three months pregnant at the time William married her. (It is ironic to note that Shakespeare and his wife named their daughter after a biblical character who spurns the sexual advances of a man and maintains her chastity.) Two years later in February 1585, Anne Shakespeare gave birth again, this time to twins, Hamnet, a boy, and Judith, a girl.

William seems to have regretted his early marriage in his later life, and his plays contain many references that seem to be criticisms of his own youthful misadventures. In *A Midsummer Night's Dream*, Lysander tries to talk his way into Hermia's bed, saying "One turf shall serve as pillow for us both, / One heart, one bed, two bosoms, and one troth." Hermia turns him away, telling him to "Lie further off, in humane modesty; / Such separation as may well be said / Becomes a virtuous bachelor and a maid."[8] In *The Tempest*, Prospero (a thinly disguised Shakespeare) warns Ferdinand against premarital sex with his daughter:

If thou dost break her virgin-knot before
All sanctimonious ceremonies may
With full and holy rite be minist'red,
No sweet aspersion shall the heavens let fall
To make this contract grow; but barren hate,

William Shakespeare and his wife, Anne Hathaway. Shakespeare married at eighteen and became a father when Anne gave birth to their first daughter six months later.

Sour-ey'd disdain, and discord shall
   bestrew
The union of your bed with weeds
   so loathly
That you shall hate it both.[9]

Needless to say, it is impossible to know whether the feelings expressed by his characters reflect Shakespeare's feelings toward his own life. Scholars do know that Shakespeare settled into family life and lived up to his family obligations. Even when he was living ten months out of the year in London, he sent money home and made sure his family was provided for.

It is generally accepted that William Shakespeare worked as an apprentice in his father's glove shop until the birth of his twin children in 1585. It stands to reason that, faced with a new wife and three hungry mouths to feed, Shakespeare would keep the job he had been employed in since leaving grammar school. However, after 1585, Shakespeare fades from sight until he resurfaces in London in 1592 as the object of a scathing attack by Robert Greene.

Many biographers of Shakespeare refer to 1585 to 1592 as the "Lost Years." Because of the lack of records, speculation

The Lost Years

"From the date of the twins' christening until his emergence in London seven years later as the target of an attack by a fellow writer, Robert Greene, the records of Shakespeare are blank. Again, myths, legends, and fanciful speculations . . . [tell] about young William being in so much trouble for deer-stealing from the park at Charlecote, home of the Lucy family, that he had to leave Stratford and hide in London. Another company follows John Aubery at the end of the 17th century, recording in his *Brief Lives* that Shakespeare 'had been in his younger yeares a Schoolmaster in the Countrey.' The Roman Catholic cause and speculation about these 'lost years' come together in suggestions that he was an assistant teacher to a Lancashire Catholic household. Like so much else that has been put forward, the idea does not stand up to rigorous examination.

Yet in its way, this tantalizing seven-year gap is rather attractive, allowing everyone to construct an apprenticeship to his or her own mind, unfettered by the inconvenience of recorded fact. So Shakespeare, on the evidence of his apparently extraordinary inside knowledge, has been in the army, a lawyer's office, at sea, and so on. In the glass of those 'lost years' you see what you want to see: no bad way to approach so universal an artist. Some have him, attractively, in northern Italy (of which he has, of course, extraordinary inside knowledge—extraordinary, in fact, in that it is so often wrong) and my own favorite, frankly imaginative, has him roaming Italy as an impressionable young man trying to get on with writing the epic he knows he was born to write, but for ever distracted, not least by a company of *commedia dell' arte* players."

No records exist for seven years of Shakespeare's youth. Many historians have theorized about what he may have done during this period.

and myth have been quick to step in. Most scholars favor the idea of Shakespeare spending the Lost Years apprenticed to an acting company. Indeed, in 1587, five acting companies visited Stratford. Two of them, the Queen's Men and Leicester's Men, needed men. Although there is no evidence to support this, it is not beyond belief that a restless William Shakespeare asked a visiting company for employment and that the company, seeing the young man's intelligence and quick wit, agreed to take him on as a hired man or apprentice.

For Shakespeare, employment with an acting troupe was a step up the economic ladder: The troupes paid better than any other job available to him. There are as many different opinions on how he spent the Lost Years as there are Shakespeare scholars to argue them. Various researchers have asserted that he worked as a teacher, a sailor, a soldier, a lawyer's assistant, or traveled in northern Italy during the Lost Years. However Shakespeare spent the Lost Years, one thing is certain: He somehow found his way to London.

Chapter

2 The Early Years in London

Shakespeare came to London on "Such [a] wind as scatters young men through the world / To seek their fortunes farther than at home, / Where small experience grows."[10] And indeed, it was in London where William Shakespeare made his fortune. However, the London of Elizabethan England was different from the London of today, and it was a far cry from the country town of Stratford-upon-Avon.

Like Stratford, London sat on a riverbank, but there the similarity ended. London did not have wide, clean lanes, but narrow streets teeming with filth and life. A contemporary of Shakespeare's, Thomas Dekker, wrote:

> In every street, carts and coaches make such a thundering as if the world ran upon wheels. At every corner, men, and women, and children meet in such shoals that posts are set up . . . to strengthen the houses, lest with jostling one another they should shoulder them down. Besides, hammers are beating in one place, tubs hooping in another, pots clinking in a third, water tankards running at a tilt in a fourth. Here are porters sweating under burdens, their merchant's men bearing bags of money. Chapmen [peddlers] (as if they were leapfrog) skip out of one shop

and into another. Tradesmen . . . are lusty at legs and never stand still.[11]

Renaissance London was enclosed on three sides by the city walls and on the fourth side by the River Thames, which hosted all kinds of seagoing vessels. London was home to about 160,000 people (a small city by modern standards but huge for the time) who crowded into tenements built so close together that in some parts of the city the buildings blocked out the sun and kept the streets below in constant shadow. London Bridge, crowded with shops, spanned the Thames to the area south of London known as Bankside.

London was a metropolis in more ways than one. It was the home of a thousand entertainments. A person could attend fencing exhibitions, boxing matches (with no gloves), and public executions. For those who favored the violence of animals to the violence of men, there were arenas specializing in bear-baiting (a "sport" where a chained bear fights off a pack of dogs) and cockfights. There were merchants selling everything from apples to yarn, including the latest imports from India and America: tea and tobacco. For people who preferred the sins of the flesh there were hundreds of taverns, and thousands of prostitutes. However, the thing

The city of London as it appeared during the time Shakespeare lived and worked there. London Bridge is to the right, spanning the River Thames.

that impressed most travelers about London was not in the city itself but in a field a short distance north of the city walls in an area known as Shoreditch.

It was in Shoreditch that James Burbage, in 1576, built a round, three-story building, and named it the Theatre—it was the first time that word had been used in English to refer to a public place for plays. Burbage had to establish his Theatre outside of the jurisdiction of the city authorities because

> city officials, who considered the bands of players irresponsible vagrants, instigators of unrest, and ringleaders of riotousness, were constantly trying to prohibit the actors from playing in the innyards or bearyards (which were within their jurisdiction), put them out of business, and throw them out of London.[12]

Acting troupes had such a bad reputation that they had to have the patronage of nobles in order to avoid persecution. To show their appreciation, the acting companies named themselves after their patrons, such as the "Queen's Men" or the "Lord Chamberlain's Men."

Despite the ill will of city officials and because of the favor of Queen Elizabeth and her court, the theater business boomed and more theaters were built. Down the road from Burbage's Theatre, another theater, called the Curtain, was erected. Meanwhile, south of the city and across the Thames in an area known as Bankside, two more theaters, the Rose and the Swan, opened. One visitor to London wrote that "Without [outside] the city are some theaters where English actors almost every day represent tragedies and comedies to very numerous audiences; these are concluded

The Ill Repute of Players

Actors have long been a part of English culture, but they have not always enjoyed the best of reputations with the civic authorities. The authorities considered the wandering drama companies public nuisances and passed laws against them. The following two passages are from Levi Fox's The Shakespeare Handbook. *The first passage is a quote from the 1572 Act for the Punishment of Vagabonds:*

"All and every person being whole and mighty in body and able to labour, having not land or master, nor using any lawful merchandise, craft or mystery whereby he or she might get his or her living, and can give no reckoning how he or she doth lawfully get his or her living; and all fencers, bear-wards, common players in interludes and minstrels not belonging to any Baron of this realm or towards any other honourable personage of greater degree; all jugglers, pedlars, tinkers and petty chapmen [merchants], shall wander abroad and have not license of two justices of the peace at the least, whereof one be the quorum, when and in what shire they shall happen to wander . . . shall be taken, adjudged and deemed rogues, vagabonds and sturdy beggars."

It was not long after the passage of this law that James Burbage wrote the following letter to Robert Dudley, earl of Leicester, asking for continued patronage:

"We therefore, your humble servants and daily orators your players, for avoiding all inconvenience that may grow by reason of the said statute, are bold to trouble your lordship with this our suit, humbly desiring your honour that, as you have always been our good lord and master, you will now vouchsafe to retain us at present as your household servants and daily waiters, not that we crave any further stipend or benefit at your lordship's hands but our liveries as we have had, and also your honour's license to certify that we are your household servants when we shall have occasion to travel amongst our friends as we do usually once a year, and as other nobleman's players do and have done in time past, whereby we may enjoy our faculty in your lordships name as we have done heretofore."

A Midsummer Night's Dream *is performed during Shakespeare's time. The acting profession did not enjoy the best of reputations during the 1500s.*

with excellent music, variety of dances, and the great applause of the audience."[13]

It was an exciting time to be in London, and Shakespeare arrived just as the revolution in drama was taking shape. Christopher Marlowe had written his highly successful *Tamburlaine the Great* in which he married poetry to drama. Marlowe's plays first used blank verse in English drama, and it is to Marlowe that Shakespeare owes the greatest debt for his later success. One writer has observed that Marlowe "was the originating genius"[14] and that Shakespeare merely capitalized upon the achievements of Marlowe.

Marlowe and his college-educated fellows the "University Wits" were Shakespeare's primary competition. The University Wits were a group of scholarly playwrights who were famous for their experimental plays that bridged the gap between the classical and the popular dramatic traditions. The University Wits' most famous member was Christopher Marlowe, but the group also included Thomas Kyd (from whom Shakespeare would get the idea for *Hamlet*), John Lyly, George Peele, Robert Greene (who is, ironically, famous as the first person to criticize Shakespeare), and Thomas Middleton. Some of the greatest names in English literature lived during Shakespeare's life: Ben Jonson; Sir Philip Sidney; Edmund Spenser; Sir Walter Raleigh; Mary Sidney, countess of Pembroke; Michael Drayton; John Donne; and Francis Bacon. Shakespeare knew some of these people, if not all of them.

Against these intellectual giants William Shakespeare, the son of a glover, made his mark. It is thought that around 1589 Shakespeare joined, or somehow became associated with, the combined companies of Lord Strange's Men and the Admiral's Men. Although there are records of him acting, it is unlikely he was a star actor: At twenty-five years of age he was too old to play female roles (since women were forbidden by law from acting, young boys played the female roles), and too old to begin an apprenticeship. It is likely that he got his start in the theater as a hired man, probably as a "bookkeeper." Like a modern stage manager, it was the job of the bookkeeper to make sure that things ran smoothly during a performance.

The bookkeeper's most important responsibility was to keep the company's "playbook." Since copyright laws did not exist at the time, each company kept secret the texts of the plays they performed. It was the bookkeeper's duty to buy plays, to

A member of the "University Wits," Christopher Marlowe wrote many successful dramas in London. Marlowe and his colleagues were Shakespeare's competitors.

get the appropriate license from the Revels Office (the government censor), and to revise the plays according to the actors' criticisms, the troupe's needs, and the government's standards. It was also the bookkeeper's function to copy out the parts for the actors. It is from his experience as a bookkeeper that Shakespeare developed his keen dramatic instinct. It is likely that this background, and the added financial opportunity that playwriting offered, led to Shakespeare composing his own plays. It would allow him to get paid twice: once as a writer, and then again as bookkeeper. Shakespeare the businessman was always on the lookout for extra income.

William Shakespeare became a force in Elizabethan drama with the popularity of his first four history plays: *Henry VI* (Parts 1, 2, and 3) and *Richard III*. Drawing his inspiration from Holinshed's *Chronicles,* this tetralogy covers the events leading up to, and including, the War of the Roses. The plays examine a country in turmoil, split by loyalties to rival kings and a nobility out of control. The War of the Roses ends with the death of Richard III and the crowning of Henry VII as king, thus beginning the Tudor dynasty of which Queen Elizabeth was a product. One critic has observed of the character of Richard III:

> He is both the instrument and the victim of Divine justice: his reign is a punishment on the country for the War of the Roses, and his death a punishment for his reign; Richmond's victory, and his accession as the first Tudor monarch Henry VII, is a sign that God's wrath is assuaged.[15]

There can be little doubt that such flattering treatment of Queen Elizabeth's family captured her notice.

Many of Shakespeare's plays were based on events in English history. These plays, which include those based on the lives of Henry VI and Richard III, were tremendously popular in Shakespeare's own time.

Shakespeare was also capitalizing on public opinion. Written and performed between 1589 and 1593, the tetralogy is a celebration of national pride. In 1588, the Spanish Armada had been defeated despite overwhelming odds. In 1591, an army under the command of Robert Devereux, earl of Essex, was sent to France to help the Protestant Henry of Navarre win the French crown. Patriotism in England was at a high, and audiences were thrilled to see the history of their country acted out on the stage. Thomas Nashe, a University Wit and rival playwright, wrote in reference to Shakespeare's *1 Henry VI:*

> How would it have joyed brave Talbot [a character in *1 Henry VI*] (the terror of the French) to think that after he

Queen Elizabeth, pictured here with her royal entourage, loved the theater and actively supported London's playwrights.

had lain two hundred years in his tomb, he should triumph again on the stage, and have his bones new embalmed with the tears of ten thousand spectators at least, (at several times) who in the tragedian [actor] that represents his person, imagine they behold him fresh bleeding.[16]

William Shakespeare's theatrical success did not escape the notice of his rival playwrights, and at least one of them did not share Nashe's enthusiasm. Another playwright, Robert Greene, called Shakespeare

an upstart crow, beautified with our feathers, that with his Tygers heart wrapt in a Player's hide, supposes he is

as well able to bombast out a blank verse as the best of you: and being an absolute Johannes Factotum [a jack-of-all-trades], is in his own conceit the only Shake-scene in a country.[17]

Although Greene does not mention Shakespeare by name, it is nonetheless obvious that Shakespeare is the target of his anger. He puns on a line from *3 Henry VI* ("Tigers heart wrapt in a player's hide" instead of "O tiger's heart wrapt in a woman's hide"[18]), and on Shakespeare's name ("Shake-scene"). Greene's anger stems from his belief that Shakespeare, since he lacked a university education, was an inferior writer compared to Greene and his fellow University Wits. Greene believed that university-educated writers were better than "those puppets [actors] . . . that spake from our mouths"[19] and was upset that an outsider, like Shakespeare, who was not only undereducated but an actor as well, should be praised by both the nobility and the masses.

Greene died before he could see his comments published, but that did not mean his attack went unanswered. A man

Elizabethan Theater

Going to the theater in Renaissance England was different from going to the theater today. The following account of a typical Elizabethan theater is from the diary of a Swiss doctor, Thomas Platter, who visited England in 1599. It is reprinted here as it appears in S. Schoenbaum's William Shakespeare: A Compact Documentary Life.

"On another occasion, also after dinner, I saw a play not far from our inn, in the suburb, at Bishopsgate, as far as I remember. . . . At the end they danced, too, very gracefully, in the English and the Irish mode. Thus every day around two o'clock in the afternoon in the city of London two and sometimes even three plays are performed at different places, in order to make people merry; then those who acquit themselves best have also the largest audience. The places are built in such a way that they act on a raised scaffold, and everyone can well see everything. However, there are separate galleries and places, where one sits more pleasantly and better, therefore also pays more. For he who remains standing below pays only one English penney, but if he wants to sit he is let in at another door, where he gives a further penney; but if he desires to sit on cushions in the pleasantest place, where he not only sees everything well but can also be seen, then he pays at a further door another English penney. And during the play food and drink is carried around among the people, so that one can also refresh oneself for one's money.

The play-actors are dressed most exquisitely and elegantly, because of the custom in England that when men of rank or knights die they give and bequeath almost their finest apparel to their servants, who, since it does not befit them, do not wear such garments, but afterwards let the play-actors buy them for a few pence.

How much time they [the people] thus can spend merrily every day at plays everyone knows well who has ever seen them [the actors] act or play."

by the name of Henry Chettle published the criticism of Shakespeare after Greene's death in a pamphlet called *Green's Groatsworth of Wit.* Sometime between the publication of *Green's Groatsworth of Wit* in 1592 and the publication of Chettle's own book *Kind-Heart's Dream* in 1593, Chettle met William Shakespeare. The meeting made an impression on Chettle because in the preface to his own book he apologizes for the attack:

> Myself have seen his demeanour no less civil than he excellent in the quality he professes: besides, divers of worship have reported, his uprightness of dealing, which argues his honesty, and his facetious [polished] grace in writing, that approves his art.[20]

In any case, the attack had little effect on Shakespeare's growing popularity. He began to write plays at the rate of about two a year. Following the success of his historical tetralogy, Shakespeare began to expand his creative horizons beyond dramatizing his country's history. During this period he wrote *Titus Andronicus* and *The Comedy of Errors,* his first tragedy and comedy.

Titus Andronicus is heavily influenced by both the gory tragedies of the Roman playwright Seneca and the writings of the Roman poet Ovid (both of whom Shakespeare studied in grammar school). *Titus* was extremely popular on the Renaissance stage and contains elements that can be found in any modern horror movie: rape, dismemberment, death, and cannibalism. Because of its bloody nature, many people have claimed that it was not written by Shakespeare, but the experts now agree that it is Shakespeare's handiwork. One critic has observed of *Titus Andronicus* that

"The pattern of revenge and madness is similar in *Hamlet,* while the patriarch who precipitates his own downfall and the degeneration of his society recurs in *King Lear.*"[21]

Shakespeare's first comedy is as ambitious as his first tragedy. Employing the age-old device of mistaken identities (old even in Shakespeare's time), *The Comedy of Errors* revolves around sex, money, and slapstick violence (like many modern comedies). The play is interesting because of Shakespeare's adherence to the Greco-Roman unities of time (the action of the play lasts as long as the performance), place (the action takes place in a single imaginary location), and action (no subplots). The only other play that obeys the unities is Shakespeare's "farewell" play, *The Tempest,* which was written near the end of his career. *The Comedy of Errors* shows Shakespeare moving "towards the more fluid and less plot-bound form of romantic comedy which he was to develop"[22] in his later comedies.

Things were going well for the budding playwright when disaster struck. From 1592 to 1594, the plague ravished London, killing almost eleven thousand people. The cries "Bring out your dead" echoed through the streets on a daily basis as carts traveled around the city collecting the previous night's dead. Those who could afford to leave the unhealthy air of the city for the country did so, while those who could not had to remain. In order to combat the plague, the public theaters were closed. "We think it fit," the royal order reads, "that all manner of concourse and public meetings of the people at plays, bear-baitings, bowlings and other like assemblies for sports be forbidden . . . whereby no occasions be offered to in-

A victim of the Black Plague is attended by a physician. The plague swept Europe from 1592 to 1594, infecting and killing countless victims. In an attempt to stop the continuing spread of infection, theaters were closed in England and Shakespeare was suddenly unemployed.

crease the infection within the city." [23] The closing of the public theaters put Shakespeare out of work, and he was forced to earn a living by different means.

In 1593, during the worst of the plague, Shakespeare published his first book. The slim volume contained the poem "Venus and Adonis," an erotic narrative written in the style of Shakespeare's rival, Christopher Marlowe. The poem tells the story of a youth, Adonis, who rejects the advances of the goddess of love, Venus. It is ironic to note that, while this poem is largely ignored today, this first work of Shakespeare's invention was the most popular thing he wrote in his own day. In an amateur play of about the same time, one of the characters remarks: "Let this dunci-fied world esteem of Spencer and Chaucer, I'll worship sweet Mr. Shakespeare, and to

honour him will lay his 'Venus and Adonis' under my pillow." One biographer has noted that "Multitudes bought 'Venus and Adonis'; the poem went through sixteen editions before 1640. No other work by Shakespeare achieved so many printings during this period. Readers thumbed it until it fell to pieces." [24]

The sequel to "Venus and Adonis" was published the following year in 1594. Although it never attained the popularity of "Venus and Adonis," "The Rape of Lucrece" nonetheless went on to be reprinted several times before 1640. In contrast to "Venus and Adonis," "The Rape of Lucrece" tells the story of a young man's successful seduction of an older woman. Although both "Venus and Adonis" and "The Rape of Lucrece" are today considered inferior to his plays, the two poems

The Groundlings

In the following passage from The Shakespeare Handbook, *a modern historian discusses the accuracy of the idea that the "groundlings" were ignorant audience members who only attended plays to disrupt them:*

"It is often assumed that the poorer members of the audience who stood in the yard area around the stage were unruly and ignorant. The 'groundlings' who paid the cheapest entry fee of one penney, so the argument goes, were inclined to interrupt plays they disapproved of by jeering, cracking nuts, hurling fruit at the stage, and generally upstaging the players with their boorish behavior. These 'stinkards,' as they are sometimes referred to, apparently passed their afternoons being bored and confused by the greater part of the plays they watched, waiting for some 'comic business,' 'light relief,' or horror effect to amuse them. This view seems to be based mainly on snobbery about the 'lower orders' backed up by a few comments from the period taken out of context. Thus Hamlet's famous complaint about the groundlings who are 'capable of nothing but inexplicable dumb shows and noise' is sometimes cited to prove that much of the audience was rather moronic. I do not wish to give the impression that the audience was necessarily reverent or particularly 'well-behaved' in the way that we might describe a quiet and respectful bourgeois [middle-class] audience at the theater today. However it does seem unlikely that people would regularly pay a substantial amount of their income to see plays which they found incomprehensible."

tell us something about the man writing them. During this period of his life, with the public theaters closed, William Shakespeare tried to make a living by writing poetry calculated to appeal to a select audience: university students, courtiers, lawyers, and above all, the nobility.

"Venus and Adonis" and "The Rape of Lucrece" were both dedicated to the nineteen-year-old earl of Southampton, Henry Wriothesley. The reason for the dedication is simple: money. With the public theaters closed because of the plague, Shakespeare was effectively out of work as a playwright. By dedicating his "unpolished lines to your Lordship,"[25] Shakespeare was hoping to secure patronage from the young earl. The tradition of patronage was a holdover from the medieval era when artists of all kinds (poets, painters, singers, actors) were dependent upon the nobility for their livelihoods. The nobles gave money to the artists in return for performances and works of art.

The relationship between Southampton and William Shakespeare is unclear, but it is certain that Southampton provided Shakespeare with some type of support during the plague years. Critics cite the difference in tone between the two dedications as evidence of this. One critic has described the dedication of "Venus and Adonis" as "elaborately courteous but not servile, self-deprecatory but with an undertow of confidence—[arguing] no great intimacy between poet and patron." Those same critics see "a progression of warmth"[26] in the later dedication of "The Rape of Lucrece" to Southampton, which is assumed to come from a growing friendship between the two men. Nicholas Rowe, one of Shakespeare's earliest biographers, tells of

> one instance so singular in the magnificence of this patron of Shakespeare's . . . that my Lord Southampton, at one time, gave him [Shakespeare] a thousand pounds, to enable him to go through with a purchase which he heard he had a mind to.[27]

Although the amount here is unrealistic (at the time of his death, Shakespeare's combined holdings were not worth a thousand pounds), there is little doubt that Henry Wriothesley, earl of Southampton, contributed in some way to Shakespeare's livelihood. Scholars believe that Southampton gave Shakespeare the money he needed to buy an interest in the Lord Chamberlain's Men when it reformed after the plague abated.

At about the same time that Shakespeare wrote and published "Venus and Adonis" and "The Rape of Lucrece," he began work on his famous series of sonnets. A sonnet is a rhymed, fourteen-line poem made famous by the Italian poet Petrarch. Sonnets are typically written in a "cycle," or series, so that the poems tell a story. Generally, the poems celebrate the undying love of the poet for his beloved, usually a woman, by listing her beauties and virtues in ornate language. Shakespeare's sonnets are unusual and famous because of their variation on this tradition. Even though Shakespeare began to write the sonnets in 1593, the cycle was not completed until 1595, and it remained unpublished until 1609 when a pirated version was finally printed.

After the theaters in London closed, Shakespeare sought and found a patron for his poetry, Earl of Southampton Henry Wriothesley (pictured). Although it is unknown how much money Wriothesley gave Shakespeare, it is certain that he supported the writer to some extent.

The first 126 poems are addressed to a "Young Man" of superior beauty and social rank, and they alternately encourage him to marriage and scold him for his shortcomings. The poems celebrate not homosexual lust, but the platonic love of one man for another. The sonnets numbered 127 to 152 involve the poet's mistress, the mysterious "Dark Lady." The poet's attitude toward her is openly sexual but turns to revulsion after he examines his conscience, and learns that the Dark Lady has left him for the Young Man of the earlier sonnets. Several poems throughout the cycle refer to a third character, nicknamed the "Rival Poet" by literary critics, who is competing with the "Older Poet" of the sonnets for the Young Man's affection. The story that Shakespeare's sonnets tell is one of love, betrayal, and competing affections.

Was Shakespeare an Adulterer?

Was Shakespeare faithful to his wife? Probably not. The following passage from Edmund Chambers's A Short Life of Shakespeare with the Sources *describes one friend giving another friend a hard time about a failed love affair (the two friends are supposedly Henry Wriothesley, earl of Southampton, and William Shakespeare):*

"H. W. being suddenly infected with contagion of a fantasticall fit [love], at the first sight of A, pineth a while in secret grief, at length not able to endure the burning heate of so fervent a humour, bewrayeth [betray] the secrecy of his disease unto his familiar friend W. S. who not long before had tryed the curtsey of the like passion, and was now newly recovered of the like infection; yet finding his friend let blood in the same vaine, he took pleasure for a time to see him bleed, & instead of stopping the issue, he enlargeth the wound, with the sharp razor of willing conceit, persuading him that he thought it a matter very easy to be compassed, & no doubt with pain, diligence & some cost in time obtained. Thus this miserable comforter comforting his friend with an impossibility, either for that he could now secretly laugh at his friend's folly, that had given occasion not long before unto other to laugh at his owne, or because he would see whether an other could play his part better than himself, & in viewing a far off the course of this loving Comedy, he determined to see whether it would sort to a happier end for this new actor, then it did for the old player. But at length this Comedy was like to have grown to a Tragedy, by the weake & feeble estate that H. W. was brought unto, by a desperate view of an impossibility of obtaining his purpose."

The temptation to read the sonnets as autobiography is great and has caused at least one biographer to comment that "More folly has been written about the sonnets than about any other Shakespearean topic."[28] Although the Older Poet of the cycle is undoubtedly Shakespeare, there is a great deal of argument as to how much of the subject matter is drawn from his life and how much is pure invention. The Young Man has been variously identified but is likely Shakespeare's patron, the earl of Southampton. This is a reasonable assumption given that Shakespeare began to write the sonnets at roughly the same time as he was trying to secure Southampton's patronage. This also throws light upon the shadowy Rival Poet who is vying for the Young Man's affection. Shakespeare was not alone in trying to win Southampton's favor. Both Thomas Nashe and Christopher Marlowe had dedicated poems to the young nobleman in the hope of securing his patronage. The Dark Lady, Shakespeare's most enigmatic figure, continues to defy identification. Many books have been written speculating on her true identity, but all that remains clear is that if she ever existed, she provided Shakespeare with the inspiration for some of his best poetry.

Whatever the case may be, this phase of Shakespeare's life soon came to an end. In 1594, the plague eased and the public theaters reopened. No longer obliged to seek his livelihood from noble patrons, Shakespeare turned again to the stage and playwriting as a means of employment.

3 The Lord Chamberlain's Men

When the plague that had been ravishing London for two years finally loosened its grip on the city, Shakespeare went back to work. The upper classes, who had fled the deadly city for the healthy countryside, were returning. Everyone, from the humblest apprentice to the greatest lord, was starving for entertainment after the horror of the plague.

After the plague, Shakespeare bought a share (probably with money from Southampton) in the reformed Lord Chamberlain's Men and joined his friends Richard Burbage and William Kemp. He had worked with both men prior to the plague (show business then, as now, involved many temporary alliances between actors and producers); 1594 is the earliest date for the three of them working together. The records of the treasurer of the queen's chamber contain an entry that records payment to the three men for two royal performances at Greenwich in 1594. The alliance between Richard Burbage (who would come to embody the roles of Hamlet, Othello, and King Lear) and William Shakespeare would last for the rest of Shakespeare's life (William Kemp eventually bowed out of the company and went his own way).

The year 1594 is also notable for a riotous performance of *The Comedy of Errors*

on December 28 at Gray's Inn, the largest of the four Inns of Court where young gentry went to study law. In their free time these young gentlemen would amuse themselves with drinking, gambling, chasing ladies, and, on a higher level, literature and theatricals. Too many invitations had

When London's theaters reopened, Shakespeare bought a share in the Lord Chamberlain's Men and joined his close friend Richard Burbage (pictured). Burbage also played several leading roles in Shakespeare's plays.

James Burbage

James Burbage is considered to be the father of English drama: He established the first public theater (called the Theatre) in 1576, and his son Richard went on to become a famous actor who popularized the characters William Shakespeare created. The following passage from A. L. Rowse's book Shakespeare the Man *discusses the alliance between the Burbages and Shakespeare:*

"The Burbages took the lead in the organisation of a new company under the Lord Chamberlain's own aegis [protection]. . . . William Shakespeare was next in importance to the Burbages themselves, the creators of the enterprise; in the documents his name appears first; he must have taken a leading part in the new venture. He could bring to it his skill as an actor, the plays he had written—and those he was going to write, henceforth exclusively for the company—perhaps his social contacts and graces, which James Burbage was without. Burbage, more than thirty years older, had begun life as a joiner, then turned to playing; when he built the first theatre and the Curtain out in the Liberty of Holywell in Shoreditch his carpentry must have come in handy. He had begun life poor; he was a tough customer, as he needed to be, rude and not overly honest in earlier days. He had two sons, Cuthbert and Richard, who became the star of the Company. All three Burbages were entirely theatre-men: no other business . . . no one could have foretold that the combination of the Burbages with Shakespeare would achieve first place, let alone attain such continuous success."

been sent out and accepted for the yuletide festivities that first year after the plague. The audience was so rowdy drinking and flirting with women that Shakespeare's actors could not perform. In the end

> it was thought good not to offer anything of account, saving dancing and revelling with gentlewomen; and after such sports, a *Comedy of Errors* (like to Plautus his *Menechmus*) [the source of Shakespeare's play] was played by the players. So that night was begun, and continued to the end, in nothing but confusion and errors; whereupon, it was ever afterwards called, The Night of Errors.[29]

Starting in 1594, Shakespeare became the "ordinary poet" for the Lord Chamberlain's Men, which meant that he was their regular playwright. Professional is the best word to describe Shakespeare during this period. Only a few writers during Shakespeare's life were as prolific as he was, especially during the 1594–1596 period. His plays display the poetic skills he developed during the plague while he was writing the

William Shakespeare completed four comedies between the years 1594 and 1596. Two of these, The Taming of the Shrew *and* A Midsummer Night's Dream, *remain popular today.*

sonnets and the poems for the earl of Southampton. Shakespeare was beginning to develop the dramatic technique that would reach perfection in his later tragedies and romances.

Shakespeare also wrote four comedies between 1594 and 1596: *The Taming of the Shrew, The Two Gentlemen of Verona, Love's Labor's Lost,* and the fanciful *A Midsummer Night's Dream. The Taming of the Shrew* tells the story of Katherina the Shrew (a "shrew" is an ill-tempered scolding woman) who is "tamed" by her new husband and turned into a model wife. This theme was a com-

mon one in Shakespeare's day, but Shakespeare's depiction of a woman's humiliation was so controversial in his own time that it has the dubious honor of being the only play by Shakespeare that provoked a dramatic "response" by another playwright in his own lifetime. In John Fletcher's *The Woman's Prize or the Tamer Tamed,* Fletcher (who would collaborate with Shakespeare later in life) resurrects Shakespeare's Petruchio as a widower who remarries and is himself tamed by his second wife. *The Taming of the Shrew* continues to explore the ideas of disguise and transformation that

Did Shakespeare Hate Women?

Many feminist scholars believe that Shakespeare disliked women and point to The Taming of the Shrew *as evidence. In the following passage from* The Taming of the Shrew, *Kate (the play's "shrew"), after being "tamed" by her husband, describes the proper role of the wife:*

"A woman mov'd is like a fountain troubled,
  Muddy, ill-seeming, thick, bereft of beauty,
    And while it is so, none so dry or thirsty
  Will deign to sip, or touch one drop of it.
Thy husband is thy lord, thy life, thy keeper,
Thy head, thy sovereign; one that cares thee,
  And for thy maintenance; commits his body
    To painful labor, both by sea and land;
To watch the night in storms, the day's in cold,
Whilst thou li'st warm at home, secure and safe;
  And craves no other tribute at thy hands
  But love, fair looks, and true obedience—
    Too little payment for so great a debt.
Such duty as the subject owes the prince,
Even such a woman oweth to her husband;
And when she is froward, peevish, sullen, sour,
  And not obedient to his honest will,
    What is she but a foul contending rebel,
  And graceless traitor to her loving lord?
I am asham'd that women are so simple
To offer war where they should kneel for peace,
  Or seek for rule, supremacy, and sway,
When they are bound to serve, love, and obey.
Why are our bodies soft, and weak, and smooth,
  Unapt to toil and trouble in the world,
But that our soft conditions, and our hearts,
  Should well agree with our external parts?
Come, come, you froward and unable worms!
My mind hath been as big as one of yours,
  My heart as great, my reason haply more,
To bandy word for word and frown for frown;
  But now I see our lances are but straws,
Our strength as weak, our weakness past compare,
That seeming to be most which we indeed least are."

Shakespeare first used in *The Comedy of Errors*. Disguise and transformation are two themes Shakespeare returns to again and again in his later works.

The Two Gentlemen of Verona is notable as Shakespeare's first attempt at romantic comedy. It contains many of the elements of the earlier plays, and more. This play marks the beginning of Shakespeare's life-long pattern of giving his female characters superiority in matters of love while the male characters are unreliable and ridiculous. Even though the play looks forward to later comedies and their focus on transformation through love, it is hopelessly flawed. Some critics argue that the text is an incomplete revision and that Shakespeare changed his mind about the locations of the play, the titles of his characters, and the conclusion.

Coming on the heels of the unpolished *Two Gentlemen of Verona*, *Love's Labor's Lost* is remarkably well thought out. This play tells the story of the king of Navarre and his three attendant lords who vow to "war against their own affections / And the huge army of the world's desires"[30] by spending three years in studying and fasting with no female companionship. As soon as the promises are made, the daughter of the king of France, coincidentally accompanied by three attendant ladies, arrives on the scene. The scene appears to be set for a conventional courtship comedy with a happy ending where everyone gets married and lives happily ever after. However, Shakespeare defies tradition by having the women fail to marry the men at the end of the play and instead has them insist upon a waiting period of one year in order to test the quality of the men's love. This play is a continuation of Shakespeare's pet theme of transformation through love.

A Midsummer Night's Dream is one of Shakespeare's most popular comedies, and it has been turned into a ballet and an opera. It contains all the devices of his earlier comedies (mistaken identities, star-crossed lovers, transformations, and disguises) plus fairies, magic, music, and song. *A Midsummer Night's Dream* is similar in many ways to a masque. A masque was a type of play popular among the nobility of the time in which members of the audi-

This title page for Shakespeare's play Love's Labor's Lost *is the earliest one bearing his name still in existence. Featuring Shakespeare's favorite theme of transformation through love, the well-conceived play was written shortly after* Two Gentlemen of Verona.

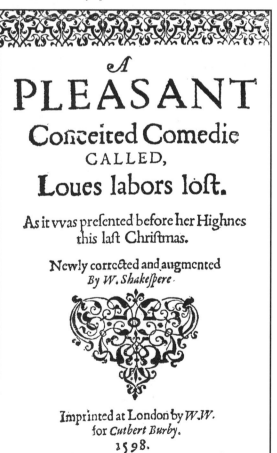

A PLEASANT Conceited Comedie CALLED, Loues labors loſt.

As it vvas preſented before her Highnes this laſt Chriſtmas.

Newly corrected and augmented By W. Shakeſpere·

Imprinted at London by W.W. for *Cutbert Burby.*
1598.

ence would put on costumes or disguises and take part in the action of the play. Masques were elaborately staged events that had not only drama but singing and dancing as well. It is generally believed that Shakespeare was commissioned to write *A Midsummer Night's Dream* for the wedding of Sir Thomas Heneage, the elderly treasurer of the chamber, to the mother of Shakespeare's patron, Mary, countess of Southampton, in May 1594.

At the same time he was exploring the limits of comedy, Shakespeare was also writing things that he knew would succeed with the public. Between 1594 and 1596, Shakespeare wrote *King John* and *Richard II*, which added two more histories to his growing repertoire. Neither of these plays is exceptional. They are both uneven in quality and explore the consequences of a weak king contending with a popular and powerful subject who wishes to win the throne. These plays would set the stage for Shakespeare's later, overwhelmingly popular *Henry IV* (Parts 1 and 2), and its epilogue, *Henry V.*

During this time, Shakespeare also wrote *Romeo and Juliet*, which was then, as now, one of his most popular plays. It tells the story of two young lovers from rival families who find each other, court, marry, and then die in each other's arms. Shakespeare was writing his sonnets at the same time he was writing *Romeo and Juliet*. The play itself contains two sonnets and might be viewed as an embodiment of the world of the love sonnet: a passionate but fragile state that collapses under the weight of reality. *Romeo and Juliet* has been produced on stage more times and in a greater variety of ways than any of Shakespeare's other plays. Although it is common to read the play as a glorification of young love (or

This drawing depicts the famous balcony scene from Romeo and Juliet. *Unmistakably one of Shakespeare's most popular plays, it has been produced more times with more variations than any other of his works.*

lust), a close reading of the play makes it clear that Shakespeare is exposing the folly of such love.

Shakespeare seems to have had a hand in rewriting plays other than his own during the 1594–1596 period. In a manuscript copy of *Sir Thomas More*, authorities believe they have the only existent copy of dramatic dialogue written in Shakespeare's actual handwriting. As a play, *Sir Thomas More* is at its best mediocre, but the value of the play is not in its dramatic content. It is interesting because it offers "us a unique view of what Shakespeare's 'foul papers' [rough drafts] may have looked like and the kinds of problems which such a copy posed for a scribe preparing a prompt-book or for an Elizabethan printer."[31] Written and rewritten by no less than six different people, the heavily revised manuscript gives us a unique window into the cooperative nature of the theater during Shakespeare's life. Originally written by one of Shakespeare's competitors, Anthony Munday, the play was passed to at least five other writers (Shakespeare included) in an attempt to rewrite it for dramatic production and to get it around the objections of the royal censor, Sir Edmund Tilney, who wanted to delete about one-quarter of the original play that dealt with a revolt by commoners.

Shakespeare's star was on the rise. Shakespeare and the Lord Chamberlain's Men first performed for Queen Elizabeth during the yuletide festivities of 1594. These two performances confirmed his status as a playwright to be reckoned with, more so because during the worst of the plague, two of his chief rivals had died. In 1593, the leading playwright, Christopher Marlowe, was killed in a brawl at a tavern, and one year later, Thomas Kyd, from whom Shakespeare borrowed the revenge tragedy and the idea for his own *Hamlet,* died probably as a result of the plague. The events of the plague years

> matured and equipped [Shakespeare]— the increased sophistication with the introduction to cultivated society [by the earl of Southampton], the refinement of the senses observable in his imagery; the artistic development with cultural contacts with other arts, in ad-

William Shakespeare became increasingly popular among the public and royal court alike. Together with the Lord Chamberlain's Men, he first played for Queen Elizabeth in 1594.

dition to literature, the deep and lasting love of music, if only a superficial acquaintance with painting. Then there was the exploration of other emotional areas of friendship, love and sex than those offered by a provincial country town.[32]

It was his friendship with the earl of Southampton during this time that allowed him to purchase a share in the newly reformed Lord Chamberlain's Men. It is commonly thought that the sum of money given by the earl to Shakespeare, as recorded by Nicholas Rowe, was used to purchase this share. For Shakespeare, this was a big step up toward middle-class respectability. No longer was he dependent upon the generosity of the nobility for his livelihood, nor was he a hired hand for the company. As a "sharer" he was entitled to share in the profits of the company's dramatic enterprises along with helping to shoulder the costs of production. He was becoming, as one critic has observed, "the most complete man of the theater of his time." [33]

Shakespeare was in fact doing so well that he realized his lifelong dream and finally became a "gentleman." During the Renaissance in England, a gentleman (or a gentlewoman) was by definition a person who was descended from a noble family either by blood or by marriage. It was one step above the status of middle-class commoner. In practice, however, the status of gentleman could be attained if one had enough money. It was possible, for exam- ple, for a baker or blacksmith without any noble bloodlines to become a gentleman if the right people were paid; a heritage would be invented. Shakespeare's heritage needed no invention. His mother was an Arden and descended from minor nobility, and his wife was a Hathaway, a family of well-respected yeomen in his native county of Warwickshire. Accordingly, John Shakespeare was awarded a coat of arms by the College of Arms in 1596 (it was traditional to award the arms to the eldest male member of the family, which, in this case, was Shakespeare's father). This award allowed Shakespeare to legally sign himself "Gentleman." A gentleman had two primary

A prosperous Shakespeare reads to Queen Elizabeth and her adoring subjects. During the height of his popularity, Shakespeare applied for and received the title of "gentleman."

The site of Shakespeare's last house as it appears today, located in a wealthy area of Stratford-upon-Avon.

advantages over a commoner: One, it confirmed class status as a member of the gentry, and two, a gentleman could testify and bring suit in court without taking an oath. It is believed that William worked behind the scenes and through his noble connections at court to secure what his father had first applied for more than twenty years before.

This piece of personal good fortune was balanced by the death of Shakespeare's only son, Hamnet, who was buried on August 11, 1596. The death of his son ended any hope Shakespeare may have had for perpetuating the family name and is the reason that no direct descendants of William Shakespeare exist today. In more ways than one, 1596 was a pivotal year in Shakespeare's life.

To reinforce his newly acquired status as a gentleman, Shakespeare bought the biggest house in Stratford-upon-Avon in 1597. Called "New Place," the house stood in the best part of Stratford across the street from the chapel and the grammar school Shakespeare had attended as a boy.

It was a large house of three stories with servants' quarters, two barns, two orchards, and a garden, but it was badly in need of repair. After making the needed renovations, Shakespeare moved his wife, Anne, and his two daughters into New Place, but he was rarely in residence himself since he spent the largest part of the year in London attending to theater business. Although business kept him away from home for the majority of the year, "Mr. William Shakespeare was wont to go into Warwickshire once a year"[34] to see his wife and children. It is ironic that as Shakespeare was securing for himself the trappings of a country gentleman in Stratford, he failed to pay his taxes in London. This failure to pay taxes has caused a few scholars to wonder about Shakespeare's financial state, and they believe that his resources were stretched to the limit at this time. However, it appears the back taxes were paid by 1600.

Shakespeare's success in the theater continued in the 1596–1597 season. He produced two works, which coincidentally

Was Shakespeare Anti-Semitic?

One of the major criticisms of Shakespeare's The Merchant of Venice *is that it is anti-Semitic. Even though Shylock the Jew is totally humiliated at the end of the play, he is the character with whom audiences identify. In this passage from the play, Shylock asks what the difference is between a Christian and a Jew:*

"He hath disgrac'd me and hind'red me half a million, laugh'd at my losses, mock'd at my gains, scorn'd my nation, thwarted my bargains, cool'd my friends, heated mine enemies; and what's his reason? I am a Jew. Hath not a Jew eyes? Hath not a Jew hands, organs, dimensions, senses, affections, passions; fed with the same food, hurt with the same weapons, subject to the same diseases, heal'd by the same means, warm'd and cool'd by the same winter and summer, as a Christian is? If you prick us, do we not bleed? If you tickle us, do we not laugh? If you poison us, do we not die? And if you wrong us, shall we not revenge? If we are like you in the rest, we will resemble you in that. If a Jew wrong a Christian, what is his humility? Revenge. If a Christian wrong a Jew, what should his sufferance be by Christian example? Why, revenge. The villainy you teach me, I will execute, and it shall go hard but I will better the instruction."

A scene from The Merchant of Venice. *The main character of the play, the contemptible Shylock, is considered to be one of Shakespeare's most memorable.*

contain his two most memorable characters. The first of these was *The Merchant of Venice.* Unlike his previous comedies, *The Merchant of Venice* was an uneasy "mixture of romantic and anti-romantic elements."[35] The story revolves around the Jew Shylock who agrees to lend his antagonist Antonio three thousand ducats on the condition that if it is not paid back within three months Antonio must forfeit "an equal pound / Of your [Antonio's] fair flesh, to be cut off and taken / In what part of your body pleaseth me."[36] By the end of the play, Shylock has lost everything: His daughter has taken all his wealth, changed her religion, and married a Christian; he loses the three thousand ducats he lent Antonio, and his pound of flesh by a technicality in the contract; and the final insult is that he is forced to give up his religion. Compared with Shakespeare's other comedies, there is nothing funny about this one. It contains all the elements of the previous comedies with a slight variation: Instead of the play ending in a marriage, the marriage takes place in the middle of the play and it ends with the women scolding their husbands for failing to keep their promises. Despite being degraded in every way by the end of the play, Shylock is considered to be one of Shakespeare's most memorable characters.

Falstaff and Success

Shakespeare turned again to history and its proven success at the box office, this time striking it big with *Henry IV Part 1.* This play, and its companion *Henry IV Part 2,* are considered Shakespeare's finest history plays. One writer has commented:

All the preceding history plays had been but a preparation for the writing of these two great masterpieces, which incorporate every strand of their predecessors into a structure of extraordinary beauty. . . . The limitless possibilities of comedy and the restrictions of historical drama are combined in unparalleled richness.[37]

The two plays narrate the transformation of the hell-raising Prince Hal into a wise and respected king. The plays shift between court, tavern, and rebel camp, and the three areas are constantly compared and contrasted. The moods of the plays alternate from festive to depressive, and contain elements of tragedy, comedy, romance, and folklore mixed in such a way as to capture the complexity of life.

As perfect as these two plays are, it is the imperfect character of Sir John Falstaff who has captured the attention of audiences throughout the centuries. Falstaff is an important character in Shakespeare's dramatic development. In the two parts of *Henry IV,* Falstaff is the fat, cowardly knight who leads the young Prince Hal into drinking, carousing, and other assorted mischief. The plays reach their climax when Prince Hal rejects Falstaff and renounces and repents his former misdeeds.

Originally named Sir John Oldcastle, the character name had to be changed to Falstaff because Shakespeare unwittingly offended a noble family who traced their lineage back to a real Sir John Oldcastle, also known as Lord Cobham. The historical Sir John Oldcastle called the pope the Antichrist and was subsequently hanged and burned for his offense by the Catholics in power at the time. However, the Protestants, who were in power during Shakespeare's time, considered the man to

An illustration from 1672 shows Sir John Falstaff (lower left-hand corner) and other characters during a performance of Henry IV. Queen Elizabeth was so taken with Falstaff that she demanded that Shakespeare write another play featuring the knight, The Merry Wives of Windsor.

be a martyr. To turn such a respected man into a clown on the public stage was unthinkable, even more so because the family still wielded power at court. A letter of the time describes the situation:

> That in Shakespeare's first show of Harrie the Fifth, the person with which he undertook to play a buffoon was not Falstaffe, but Sir John Oldcastle, and that offense being worthily taken by personages descended from his title, as peradventure by many others also who ought to have him in honorable mem-

ory, the poet was put to make an ignorant shift of abusing Sir John Fastolphe, a man not inferior of virtue though not so famous in piety as the other.[38]

Falstaff not only brought Shakespeare a minor scandal but got him noticed by Queen Elizabeth, this time for the better. After viewing both parts of *Henry IV,* the queen

> was so well pleas'd with that admirable character of Falstaff . . . that she commanded him [Shakespeare] to continue it for one play more, and to shew him [Falstaff] in love. This is said to be the occasion of his writing *The Merry Wives of Windsor.*[39]

Scholars believe that *The Merry Wives of Windsor* was written at the command of Queen Elizabeth for performance in front of the queen and her court during the Garter Feast (when new members of the Knights of the Garter were honored by the queen) on St. George's Day (Shakespeare's birthday), April 23, 1597. This is reasonable considering that one of the men made a Knight of the Garter that year was George Carey, Lord Hunsdon, also known as the Lord Chamberlain, patron of Shakespeare's acting company.

Though not the most profound of Shakespeare's comedies, *The Merry Wives of Windsor* is important for a couple of reasons. With its sharply defined roles, its contrasting comic principles, and the mixture of realism and romance, it looks forward to the later comedies and romances. As Shakespeare organized his fellow actors backstage before the premiere in front of the queen and the nobility on his thirty-third birthday, he must have realized that success was his.

4 First the Globe, Then the World

In 1598, William Shakespeare could easily call himself England's most popular playwright. The unparalleled box-office success of his history plays, most notably *Henry IV* (Parts 1 and 2), had earned him the praise that other playwrights only dreamed of. His comedies and tragedies were acclaimed by everyone from Queen Elizabeth herself down to the humblest apprentice with a penny and an afternoon to spare. This sense of achievement was reinforced by Francis Meres (a clergyman, scholar, and self-styled social critic), who praised Shakespeare extensively in his book *Palladis Tamia* and compared him to the Greco-Roman playwrights.

December 28, 1598, came to a dramatic end when the longtime theatrical home of Shakespeare and the Lord Chamberlain's Men, the Theatre, was torn down. Negotiations had been under way for some time between James Burbage, the owner of the Theatre, and Giles Allen, the man who owned the land upon which the Theatre was built. Initially Burbage agreed to an increase in rent, but when Allen demanded that possession of the playhouse revert back to him after only five years, Burbage began to look for another site. Settling upon the Blackfriars monastery, which was situated within the city walls but not subject to city authorities, Burbage committed a large sum of money toward obtaining the building and refurbishing it. But once the aristocratic residents of the fashionable district learned there was going to be a common playhouse in their midst, they protested to the Crown, who had jurisdiction over the monastery, saying that a theater would create

> a general inconvenience to all the inhabitants of the same [Blackfriars] precinct; both by reason of the great resort and gathering together of all manner of vagrant and lewd persons that, under color of resorting to plays, will come thither and work all manner of mischief, and also to the great pestering and filling up of the same precinct, if it should please God to send any visitation of sickness as heretofore hath been, for that very same precinct is already grown very populous; and besides, that the same playhouse is so near the Church that the noise of the drums and trumpets will greatly disturb and hinder both the ministers and parishioners in time of divine service and sermons.[40]

Needless to say, Burbage was not granted permission to put on performances at Blackfriars and was subsequently stuck with the property.

Early Praise for Shakespeare

By 1598,
Shakespeare's
reputation
as a dramatist
was established
to such an
extent that
he earned the
praise of
Francis Meres.
In the following
passage from
The Riverside
Shakespeare,
Meres compares
Shakespeare's
talent to those
of the Greco-
Roman poets.

"As the Greek tongue is made famous and eloquent by Homer, Hesiod, Euripides, Aeschilus, Sophocles, Pindarus, Phocylides and Aristophenes; and the Latin tongue by Virgil, Ovid, Horace . . . so the English tongue is mightily enriched, and gorgeouslie invested in rare ornaments and resplendent abiliments by sir Philip Sidney, Spenser, Daniel, Drayton, Warner, Shakespeare, Marlowe and Chapman. . . .

As the soule of Euphorbus was thought to live in Pythagoras: so the sweete wittie soule of Ovid lives in mellifluous & hony-tongued Shakespeare, witness his *Venus and Adonis,* his *Lucrece,* his sugared Sonnets among his private friends, &c.

As Plautus and Seneca are accounted the best for Comedy and Tragedy among the Latins: so Shakespeare among the English is the most excellent in both kinds for the stage; for Comedy, witnes his *Gentlemen of Verona,* his *Errors,* his *Love Labors Lost,* his *Love Labours Wonne* [an alternative title for *The Taming of the Shrew*], his *Midsummers Nights Dream,* & his *Merchant of Venice:* for Tragedy his *Richard the 2. Richard the 3. Henry the 4. King John, Titus Andronicus* and his *Romeo and Juliet.*

As Epius Stolo said, that the muses would speake with Plautus tongue, if they would speak Latin: so I say that the muses would speake with Shakespeare fine filed phrase, if they would speak English."

As Shakespeare's reputation grew, he earned praise from nobility and commoners alike. He was even likened to the creators of the Greek and Roman classics.

One setback followed another. In January 1597, James Burbage died, and his sons, Richard and Cuthbert, Shakespeare's business associates, had to find a new home for the Lord Chamberlain's Men. Then in July the Crown ordered the "final suppression of . . . stage plays"[41] and the destruction of the Shoreditch and Bankside playhouses in reaction to the treasonous play *Isle of Dogs,* which was performed at the Swan. After the theaters were closed for a few months, the authorities relented and allowed the theaters to reopen with the understanding that treasonous material would not be tolerated on the public stage. The Lord Chamberlain's Men were playing at the Curtain at the end of the year, which was located in Shoreditch down the street from the Theatre, which remained empty and unused.

Negotiations for a new lease on the Theatre were stalled between the Burbages and Giles Allen. Secure in the knowledge that "the right and interest of the said Theatre was both in law and conscience absolutely vested" in him, Allen refused to come to terms with the brothers, and made plans "to pull down the same [the Theatre], and to convert the wood and timber thereof to some better use."[42] Left with no place for their acting company to play, and losing money every day the Lord Chamberlain's Men failed to play, the brothers Burbage decided to take matters into their own hands.

The Theatre Becomes the Globe

On December 28, 1598, while Allen was away in the country enjoying the yuletide season, a small group gathered at the empty Theatre in Shoreditch under cover of darkness. The group included the widow of James Burbage; her sons, Cuthbert and Richard; their chief financial supporter, William Smith; carpenter Peter Smith; and a dozen workmen. Still furious three years later, Giles Allen describes what happened next:

Then and there, armed . . . in a very riotous, outrageous, and forcible manner, and contrary to the laws of your Highness's realm, attempted to pull down said Theatre, whereupon divers of your subjects, servants and farmers, then going about in peaceable manner to procure them to desist from that their unlawful enterprise, they, the said riotous persons aforesaid, notwithstanding procured then therein with great violence, not only then and there forcibly and riotously resisting your subjects . . . but also then and there pulling, breaking, and throwing down the said Theatre in very outrageous, violent and riotous sort, to the great disturbance and terrifying not only your subjects . . . but of divers others of your Majesty's loving subjects there near inhabiting.[43]

After dismantling the playhouse, the brothers Burbage and their "riotous" men carried the timbers through London, then ferried them across the Thames River to Bankside, just outside the southern city limits, and there constructed a beautiful playhouse, which they called the Globe.

Allen attempted to sue but got nowhere; the terms of the expired lease specifically allowed for the dismantling and moving of the playhouse. Allen owned only the land, the Burbages owned the structure and could do anything they wanted with it. Although Shakespeare is not mentioned in any of the documents relating to the incident, it is reasonable to assume that as a sharer in the Lord Chamberlain's Men, he had a vested interest in the affair and probably approved of the action since the lack of a permanent home for the troupe meant that money was coming out of his pocket as well.

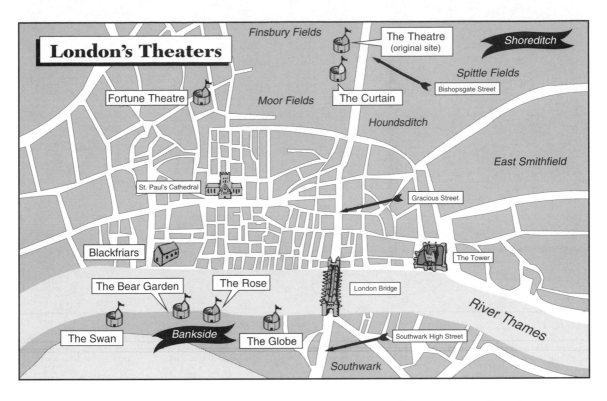

London's Theaters

Finsbury Fields
The Theatre (original site)
Shoreditch
Spittle Fields
The Curtain
Bishopsgate Street
Fortune Theatre
Moor Fields
Houndsditch
East Smithfield
St. Paul's Cathedral
Gracious Street
Blackfriars
The Tower
The Bear Garden
The Rose
London Bridge
The Swan
Bankside
The Globe
Southwark High Street
River Thames
Southwark

Since he had a financial interest in the acting company, Shakespeare scouted around for talent that would fill the seats in his theater. Acting companies always maintained relationships with outside playwrights because it was physically impossible for one man to supply a company with all the plays it needed for a year. As noted before, Shakespeare only produced two plays a year on the average. This is how William Shakespeare became acquainted with Ben Jonson.

Born in 1572, Ben Jonson was eight years younger than Shakespeare and his direct opposite. Jonson was "In complete contrast with the courtly suavity of the 'gentle' (i.e., gentlemanly) Shakespeare, who was all intuition and imagination . . . [but] Ben had the intellectualism and dogmatic bent of his Scotch ancestry."[44] Jonson had been freelancing for a rival acting

company updating plays when he came to the Curtain, where Shakespeare and the Lord Chamberlain's Men were temporarily housed, and tried to sell the company his own play, *Every Man in His Humour.* An early biographer describes the event:

Mr. Jonson, who was at that time altogether unknown to the world, had offer'd one of his plays to the players, in order to have it acted; and the persons into whose hands it was put, after having turn'd it carelessly and superciliously over, were just upon returning it to him with an ill-natur'd answer, that it would be of no service to their company, when Shakespeare luckily cast his eye upon it, and found something so well in it as to engage him first to read it through, and afterwards to recommend Mr. Jonson and his writings to

Although rival playwright Ben Jonson (pictured) constantly criticized Shakespeare, Shakespeare helped produce several of Jonson's plays and acted in two of them.

the public. After this they were profess'd friends; tho' I don't know whether the other ever made him an equal return of gentleness and sincerity.[45]

Jonson was forever criticizing Shakespeare, but as one writer has pointed out, it is "legitimate criticism by one poet of another."[46] Despite whatever criticisms Jonson had of Shakespeare, and Jonson had several, Shakespeare took Jonson under his wing and helped produce several of his plays, going so far as to act in at least two of them.

Although he is referred to as a "player" in the records of the time, Shakespeare was not known for his acting skills. The term *player* was used to refer to anyone who had anything to do with the theater: Hired men responsible for moving props and sound effects were "players" the same as the actors. Shakespeare's part in the

Lord Chamberlain's Men was more along the lines of a modern movie producer/director: He read and rewrote scripts and made sure that the actors knew their parts and that the hired men knew when certain props were to be used. Because of theater conditions at the time, an actor frequently played more than one role during any single performance, and Shakespeare was probably called upon to act from time to time in small roles. Tradition has it that he acted as king in a few of his plays as well as playing the minor, but important, roles of Adam in *As You Like It* and the Ghost in *Hamlet*.

What Shakespeare lacked in dramatic talent was made up for by the quality of the actors he hired. William Kemp was a professional clown who made famous the role of the bumbling constable Dogberry in Shakespeare's *Much Ado About Nothing*. Kemp left the Lord Chamberlain's Men in 1599 and struck out on his own, first dancing his way to Norwich and later attempting to dance his way to Rome by way of the Alps. In modern terms, Kemp was a superstar and could get employment anywhere he wanted, including at the queen's court. Then, as now, comedians were in demand. Robert Armin succeeded Kemp as clown to the Lord Chamberlain's Men. Where Kemp was a buffoon, relying more on slapstick and dirty jokes to get a laugh, Armin was "a different spirit, more subtle and intellectual with a vein of melancholy"[47] and for him Shakespeare wrote the "wise fool" roles that are a common element in his later plays, most notably in *King Lear*.

Once Shakespeare had the actors who were sure to draw audiences to his theater, he made sure to write plays that would keep the audience entertained as well as show off the talent of the acting troupe.

Between 1598 and 1602, Shakespeare wrote the plays that would once and for all secure for him the position as the playwright of the Renaissance.

Shakespeare capitalized upon the success of both parts of *Henry IV* by writing a sequel to them called *Henry V. Henry V* continues the story of Prince Hal (who was introduced in *Henry IV*) after his father, Henry IV, dies. Prince Hal becomes King Henry V and succeeds in uniting all of England and part of France under his rule. The play seems like hero worship but it in fact shows a king who is "both epic hero and fallible human . . . [who] lead[s] his country to a peace which is but the prelude to further war."[48] In many ways, *Henry V* resembles a Greek or Roman tragedy more than Shakespeare's earlier history plays, especially in its use of a chorus. A chorus was a group of singers and dancers used by the ancient playwrights to comment upon the action of the play. Shakespeare uses the chorus in *Henry V* to lend dignity to the action and to set the tone for each of the five acts.

Ben Jonson and William Shakespeare

Ben Jonson owed much to Shakespeare: Shakespeare had, after all, given Jonson a start in the theater business. But that did not keep Jonson from criticizing Shakespeare, which some people have seen as demonstrating Jonson's ingratitude. The following example of Jonson's criticism is taken from The Norton Anthology of English Literature:

"I remember the players have often mentioned it as an honor to Shakespeare that in his writing, whatsoever he penned, he never blotted out a line. My reply hath been, would he had blotted a thousand: which they thought a malevolent speech. I had not told posterity this, but for their ignorance who choose that circumstance to commend their friend by wherein he most faulted, and to justify mine own candor, for I love the man and do honor his memory, on this side of idolatry, as much as any. He was indeed honest and of an open and free nature, had an excellent fancy, brave notions, and gentle expressions, wherein he flowed with that facility that sometimes it was necessary he should be stopped: *Sufflaminandus erat* [he needed dampening], as Augustus said of Haterius. His wit was in his own power, would the rule of it had been so too. Many times he fell into those things could not escape laughter, as when he said in the person of Caesar, one speaking to him: 'Caesar, thou dost me wrong,' he replied: 'Caesar did never wrong but with just cause,' and such like, which were ridiculous. But he redeemed his vices with his virtues. There was ever more in him to be praised than to be pardoned."

Henry V closed what has since become known as the Second Tetralogy (the First Tetralogy being the three parts of *Henry VI* and *Richard III*). It should be noted that, historically, the reigns of Henry IV and Henry V (covered by Shakespeare in the Second Tetralogy) led to the kingship of Henry VI and the subsequent government of Richard III (which Shakespeare covered in the First Tetralogy). Shakespeare wrote the plays backwards, starting with the more recent history of the First Tetralogy, then moving backward in time to the events of the Second Tetralogy. After *Henry V,* Shakespeare would not come back to the history plays until the end of his career. Because of changing tastes and a changing audience (Shakespeare was, above all else, a businessman and primarily concerned with writing what would draw people to his theater), William Shakespeare began to concentrate on perfecting the tragedies and the comedies that he is known for today.

Much Ado About Nothing is a romantic comedy in which the action of the play is motivated by misunderstanding, so its title has been thought to contain a pun on the word *nothing* as *noting* (as in observation). This is an important play because it marks the first time that Shakespeare uses an "anticomic" character, or villain, in his comedies. When Don John says, "I cannot hide what I am: I must be sad when I have cause, and smile at no man's jests; eat when I have stomach, and wait for no man's leisure,"[49] it sounds very similar to Shakespeare's earlier archvillain, Richard III, when he says "I am determined to prove a villain / And hate the idle pleasures of these days . . . / . . . / As I am subtle, false, and treacherous."[50]

At the same time that *Much Ado About Nothing* was premiering on the public stage, a visitor to London, Dr. Thomas Platter of Switzerland, wrote this account of a performance of *Julius Caesar:*

> On the 21st of September [1599], after lunch, around two o'clock, I went with my companions over the water [the Thames River], [and] in the strewed roof-house [the Globe at this time had

In an old woodcut, actor William Kemp performs a dance. Kemp played the character of Dogberry in Shakespeare's romantic comedy Much Ado About Nothing.

The Globe Theatre, opened in 1599, became the stage for many of Shakespeare's plays.

a thatch roof] saw the tragedy of the first emperor Julius Caesar with fifteen characters very well acted; at the end of the comedy, in conformity with their custom, they danced with all possible grace, two dressed in men's and two in women's clothes, marvellously with one another.[51]

This account of the performance is important because it helps date the opening of the Globe (sometime previous to September 1599), and gives important clues about the staging of plays. Plays in Renaissance England were typically held in the afternoons during the weekdays and on the weekends (except for Sunday and certain feast days when the theaters were closed). Another interesting piece of information is that all the plays, whether tragedy, comedy, or history, ended with a dance in which all cast members took part. Audiences expected, and got, lavish entertainment. The theater literally had something for everyone.

In order to write *Julius Caesar*, Shakespeare drew upon the biographies of Plutarch, whom he had studied in grammar school. Because of its simple language and the skill with which the clash of ideals is depicted, *Julius Caesar* is one of Shakespeare's most popular plays. *Julius Caesar* narrates the events surrounding the assassination of the Roman emperor Julius Caesar. But beneath this historical mask, Shakespeare is examining the idea of the "divine right" of kings. The philosophy behind the divine right of kings argued that since God made kings, only God could get rid of them, and furthermore, since the king was directly chosen by God, to disobey the king and his laws was to disobey God. In *Julius Caesar*, Brutus and his henchmen come to believe that they are being ruled by a tyrant, and so they plot to kill Caesar. After Caesar's death, war and chaos take hold; the conspirators regret their decision to murder Caesar and either kill themselves or are murdered by others. It is

The Globe Theatre as it would have appeared in Shakespeare's time. The Globe had many innovative staging devices that allowed for a variety of dramatic effects.

obvious from the content of the play that Shakespeare was firmly in the corner with the idea of kings ruling by divine right (in Elizabethan England you could lose your head if you believed otherwise). *Julius Caesar* looks forward to Shakespeare's next tragedy, *Hamlet.* Brutus, with his wavering indecision about murdering Caesar, has long been thought to be a preliminary sketch for Shakespeare's finest tragic figure, Hamlet.

Coming after *Julius Caesar, As You Like It* seems like a piece of fluff in which the characters run off into the woods of Arden to escape the reality of court and town. In the forest they find the happiness they have always been searching for, get married, and live happily ever after. This, however, is an oversimplification of the play. It examines the differences between court and country, nature and fortune, youth and age, realism and romanticism, laughter and melancholy. To achieve this, Shakespeare uses the standard devices he has developed in his other comedies: mistaken identities, transformations, disguises, and an anticomic character. *As You Like It* is a play about physical and spiritual transformation, and it advances the idea that society cannot change unless the people within it change first.

Hamlet is the play that marks the beginning of Shakespeare's great tragedies. It is by far the most recognized of Shakespeare's plays—virtually everyone knows Hamlet's name and even small children know the beginning of his two most famous soliloquies thanks to Bugs Bunny: "To be, or not to be, that is the question," and "Alas, poor Yorick! I knew him." [52] The story of Hamlet had its origins in Norse myth and went through many versions written by many different people before Shakespeare got his hands on it and turned it into what has been described as "the first great tragedy Europe had produced for two thousand years."[53] It tells the story of Hamlet, the prince of Denmark, who returns home to find his father dead, poisoned by his uncle Claudius, who has married Hamlet's mother and assumed the throne of Denmark. Spurred on by the ghost of his deceased father, Hamlet agonizes throughout the play as to whether he should avenge his father's death by killing his uncle or if he should let things stand as they are. Hamlet decides upon vengeance and the play ends in a bloodbath: Not only are Hamlet and Claudius killed, but so are Hamlet's mother and just about everyone who had anything to do with the decision to kill Hamlet's father, as well as a few innocent bystanders. Shakespeare has Horatio describe the play quite accurately when he says:

> . . . you [shall] hear
> Of carnal, bloody, and unnatural acts,
> Of accidental judgements, casual
>   slaughters,
> Of deaths put on by cunning and
>   forc'd cause,
> And in this upshot, purposes mistook
> Fall'n on th' inventors' heads.[54]

Written around 1600, during the last years of Queen Elizabeth's reign, *Hamlet* indirectly deals with the question of succession. As Queen Elizabeth inched toward death people began to wonder who would succeed her, but it was such a ticklish and dangerous subject that nobody dared discuss out loud for fear of losing his head. The fact that the queen herself refused to name a successor and that Robert Devereux, earl of Essex, was beginning to talk of open rebellion and of putting himself on the throne did not help matters. England was bracing for a bloody fight for the Crown and *Hamlet* embodies this fear.

The play speaks not only to audiences of Shakespeare's time but to modern audiences as well. Many people have seen the wavering indecision of Hamlet in themselves, as poet Samuel Coleridge did when he wrote "I have a smack of Hamlet." Hamlet is often viewed as an Everyman. Apart from the Bible, *Hamlet* is one of the most quoted works in the English language. It has generated endless debates, disagreements, and commentary among not only scholars but the general public as well. *Hamlet* is such a part of Western culture

A scene from Shakespeare's Julius Caesar *shows Caesar offering his sword to Brutus. He tells Brutus to slay him if he believes that Caesar has plans to overstep his power.*

that people who know nothing else about Shakespeare know that he wrote *Hamlet*.

Written at about the same time as *Hamlet*, Shakespeare's poem "The Phoenix and the Turtle" is unique among his works. The subject of the poem is married happiness as symbolized by the phoenix, a mythical bird that was famous for its rarity (only one exists in the world at a time) and its beauty. The turtledove was renowned for its constancy in love. Some critics see the poem as depicting the relationship between Queen Elizabeth (who was often symbolically represented as a phoenix) and the rebellious earl of Essex. However, the majority of critics see the poem as a commissioned work written by Shakespeare to celebrate the long and happy marriage of Sir John Salusbury and his lady. The poem is unusual for Shakespeare because it moves from an imaginary funeral procession put on by the birds of the world to mourn the death of the phoenix and the turtledove (the ideal lovers) to an abstract argument between reason and love in which love triumphs over reason.

This was a busy time for Shakespeare because he was also at work on *Twelfth Night*. The earliest reference to Shakespeare's *Twelfth Night* is in John Manningham's diary, in which he wrote:

> At our feast we had a play called *Twelve Night or What You Will* much like *The Comedy of Errors* . . . a good practice in it to make the steward believe his lady widow was in love with him by counterfeiting a letter as from his lady in general terms telling him what she liked best in him and prescribing his gesture in smiling, his apparel etc. and then when he came to practice making him believe they took him to be mad.[55]

A painting dramatizes the play within the play from Shakespeare's Hamlet. Hamlet *is one of the most quoted works in the English language.*

Twelfth Night (*What You Will* is the alternative title given to the piece by Shakespeare) contains many of the features that are common to Shakespeare's earlier comedies: mistaken identities, disguises, transformation, an anticomic character, and an ending in which the loving couples are happily married. *Twelfth Night* falls "between the early comedies and the last romances"[56] and looks forward to the emotional quality of Shakespeare's latter plays as much as it looks back at the conventions of his earlier comedies. Many critics see the play as a bridge between Shakespeare's earlier, narrowly focused comedies and his later expansive romances.

After *Twelfth Night,* Shakespeare moved away from the strict dramatic genres of comedy, tragedy, and history. The plays written during this period of his life are called the "dark comedies" or the "problem plays" because "they are plays which critics and performers have found difficult to classify under the standard genres . . . and therefore they have felt compelled to create a new classification or genre of their own." The "problem plays" crossed genres and applied "the values of tragedy . . . to the problems of comedy"[57] and are often regarded as strange plays because they lack a strong moral conclusion.

Troilus and Cressida is the first of these "problem plays." Influenced by the works of Homer and Chaucer, Shakespeare tells the story of Troilus and Cressida's ill-fated love during the Trojan War. The characters present themselves as "honorable" and "noble," but their actions undercut these claims. The only character who emerges whole from the play is Thersites, who, as a fool, reminds us "that love is lechery, that man is animal, the body a sink of filth and diseases, and the human intellect a bad

As Queen Elizabeth grew older, the question of who would succeed her after her death arose. Hamlet *played upon the fears people had of a bloody struggle for the throne.*

joke. . . . The human condition, in his view, is faithfully mirrored in the events and personalities of the Trojan war."[58]

All's Well That Ends Well is considered by critics to be a "problem play" similar to *Troilus and Cressida. All's Well That Ends Well* concerns itself with notions of honor and how two people, Bertram and his wife, Helena, live up to, or fail to live up to, the notion of honor. Bertram, who is a noble, possesses just about every defect known to man: He is arrogant, tells lies, breaks oaths, and commits adultery. Helena, born into a lower social class than Bertram, displays all the qualities an aristocrat is supposed to possess: She is intelligent, wise, compassionate, and loyal to the extreme. By the end of the play, the audience realizes that nobility and honor are not matters of birth but a matter of intelligence and character. This topic is close to Shakespeare's heart because even though he was born a commoner he wished to be perceived as a gentleman.

Despite writing a string of hits, a growing personal fortune, and increasing recognition of his talent as a playwright, William Shakespeare's life at this point was replete with troubles. His father, John Shakespeare, died in September 1601. Described as "a merry cheeked old man" [59] who worked as a glover in his shop until he died, John Shakespeare could not have been happier with his eldest son. William Shakespeare had restored the family fortune and reputation that his father had lost, and had even realized his father's dream of securing a grant of arms that would make the Shakespeare family official members of the "gentle" class. After his father's death, Shakespeare inherited his father's home, his birthplace on Henley Street, as well as the rest of his father's estate, and he became one of the biggest landowners in Stratford-upon-Avon. Shakespeare's mother, Mary, survived her husband and lived for another seven years in the house on Henley Street with her daughter Joan and her daughter's husband, William Hart, until she died in 1608.

Whatever Shakespeare's problems may have been at home, they did not compare to the trouble that a performance of Shakespeare's *Richard II* caused in London. The problem started in 1599 when the earl of Essex had been sent to Ireland with a large army and orders from Queen Elizabeth to crush the rebel Irish forces. Essex failed miserably and returned to En-

Shakespeare's talent was increasingly recognized and rewarded after he wrote several plays that became extremely popular. But fame and fortune could not prevent trouble at home and in London.

gland against the queen's command. Irritated at his military failure and his lack of obedience, the queen ordered him detained at York House. Essex's humiliation was deepened the following year when he was privately tried for neglect of his duties, convicted, and disgraced. Instead of imprisoning him, it was decided that he would be allowed to keep his freedom because he was so popular with common people that the queen was hoping to avoid making a martyr out of him and giving her enemies a symbol to rally around.

By New Year 1601, Essex, stripped of his noble privileges and his standing at court, was at the end of his rope. "There was no future for him now so long as the Queen lived, and if she died he was ready to raise insurrection. He was the leader to whom all the irresponsible and opposition elements looked. . . . His followers were gathering around him in London for some move that was expected." On the third day of February, a meeting was held at the home of Shakespeare's former patron Henry Wriothesley, earl of Southampton. With Essex present, it was decided the group would surprise the queen and her court and that the two earls (Southampton and Essex) would capture the queen and get her under their control. The plan was that once the queen was under the control of the group, she would be forced to abdicate the throne to the earl of Essex and he would become king. Some members of the meeting thought this was too extreme and drew back at the suggestion of actually laying hands on the queen, to which Southampton, Essex's right-hand man, replied, "Shall we resolve upon nothing then?"[60] Word of the treasonous meeting leaked out and the earl of Essex was ordered to appear before the queen a few days later. He refused to go, and his fellow conspirators started to spread rumors of rebellion throughout London.

On February 7, Lord Monteagle, Sir Gelly Meyrick, Sir Joscelin, Sir Charles Percy, and other friends of the earl of Essex dined together and afterward went across the Thames to the Globe to see *Henry IV*. During the course of the play the men realized that the theater could be used to stir up the general population in favor of their friend, Essex, and his bid for the throne. To accomplish this, the men contacted the managers of the Lord Chamberlain's Men and asked that *Richard II* be played the next day in order to put the people in a rebellious mood. Testifying afterward, Augustine Phillips, a member and sharer in the acting company, said that the group had intended some other play because "that play of King Richard [was] . . . so old and so long out of use that they should have small or no company [audi-

ence] at it."[61] Shakespeare and his fellows, as conservative businessmen, were not swayed to perform the play by ideology but because the group of conspirators offered them an additional forty shillings, well above their average profit for a single play.

The ploy, and the rebellion, were complete failures. Even though the audience for the performance of *Richard II* had been stocked with sympathizers to the earl of Essex who shouted out treasonous slogans at key points in the play, the people remained unmoved. That same day, Essex and his men left Essex House and rode toward the queen's court with the intention of carrying out their plan. Upon arriving

The earl of Essex plotted to overthrow the queen and gain control of the Crown. Part of his plan included having the Lord Chamberlain's Men perform Shakespeare's play Richard II *at the Globe in an attempt to put the people of England in a rebellious mood.*

they encountered heavy resistance from the queen's retainers, and outnumbered, they retreated into London hoping to stir the common people to action. The people, however, were not as easily led as Essex had hoped, and they simply closed their windows and barred their doors against the bloody battle that they were sure was about to take place. With their attempted rebellion in disarray, Essex and his followers retreated back to Essex House and barricaded themselves in. The queen's forces surrounded Essex House, where Essex surrendered, was arrested, and was led off to London Tower (the prison at the time).

Essex and his friends were given swift trials and hanged on the twenty-fifth of February. A few of them managed to escape the hangman's noose and were confined to the tower for the rest of Queen Elizabeth's reign, including Shakespeare's old friend and patron, Southampton. The investigation after the rebellion cleared the Lord Chamberlain's Men of any intentional wrongdoing because it was thought that the promise of forty shillings was more than enough to tempt the players into performing a play that had long been out of fashion. Shakespeare and his fellows breathed a sigh of relief after being cleared by the queen because if they had been found guilty, their playhouse would have been shut down, their fortunes ruined, and they would have been executed.

Shakespeare and the Lord Chamberlain's Men played at court for the queen a day before the execution of Essex. Originally accused of playing an intentional role in Essex's plot to overthrow the queen, Shakespeare's name was cleared after further investigation.

In any case, the queen forgave them because they played at court on February 24, 1601, the day before Essex was executed. As at least one biographer has observed, "Perhaps we may credit Elizabeth's leniency . . . to her personal liking for Shakespeare's art."[62]

This rough time in Shakespeare's life was not without some good news. In May 1602, Shakespeare bought 127 acres of land in Old Stratford and a few months later bought another house in the town of Stratford. In Renaissance England, ownership of land was considered to be a measure of wealth. With his purchases of land and homes, Shakespeare was announcing to the community that he was not only a man of status but also a man of means. Shakespeare may have been rich by Renaissance standards but he was definitely not a man of leisure: Attending to his theatrical business in London, Shakespeare was unable to attend the closing of the sale in Old Stratford and left his younger brother Gilbert to take possession of the land for him.

Later that same year, Shakespeare came under attack by Ralph Brooke, York Herald for the College of Arms, for possessing a coat of arms. Brooke accused his rival in the College of Arms, Sir William Dethick, of elevating base persons and assigning devices already in use. Fourth on his list of base persons is the name of Shakespear the Player. No doubt "player" was meant as a stab at Shakespeare's right to possess a coat of arms. Nothing came of the attack and the grant of arms was sustained because of "the eligibility of John Shakespeare—a magistrate of good substance . . . who had married an heir of Arden [Shakespeare's mother, Mary]."[63]

The Death of Queen Elizabeth

The Elizabethan era came to an end on March 24, 1603, when Queen Elizabeth died at the age of seventy. A month before her death, she had her coronation ring, which symbolized her marriage to England, filed from her finger (she had worn it so long that it had become embedded in her flesh). Just before she died, she called her ministers to her and named her successor: "I will that a king succeed me, and who but my kinsman the King of Scots."[64] As soon as Queen Elizabeth died, her ministers proclaimed that James VI of Scotland would assume the throne of England as James I. With the news of her death, a sadness fell over England. Many of her subjects had never known another ruler she had reigned so long. When her hearse made its way through London for the final time, with the familiar figure of the queen crowned and sceptered, people openly wept. Thus the Tudor dynasty ended with tears for the virgin queen who had come to symbolize all that England stood for.

5 The King's Men

The arrival of King James I in 1603 marks the beginning of the Stuart dynasty, which still reigns today. The people of England were relieved by the peaceful exchange of Crowns, especially in light of the fact that just two years before the country seemed on the brink of a bloody civil war. King James I had the reputation of being merciful and just. During his month's progress from Scotland to London, James had the opportunity to demonstrate his fitness for the monarchy. At Newark-upon-Trent, on April 21, a cutpurse (pickpocket) was caught "doing the deed" in the crowd that had turned out to greet the new king. James I ordered "this silken base thief"[65] hanged, but before leaving the city, he ordered the release of all the prisoners held in the castle. These acts demonstrated to the people James's theories of how a king should govern as set forth in his book *Basilicon Doron.*

When James I arrived in London, the reception he received was muted. The plague was once again ravaging the city (30,561 deaths in one year), and those that could flee the city had already done so. As during previous visitations of the plague, the public theaters were ordered closed, but that did not stop James I from indulging his interest in drama. Within ten days of his arrival in London, James I ordered his ministers to issue a royal warrant to the Lord Chamberlain's Men that authorized

> these our servants Lawrence Fletcher, William Shakespeare, Richard Burbage, Augustyne Phillippes, John Heninges, Henrie Condell, William Sly, Robert Armyn, Richard Cowly, and the rest of their associates, freely to use and exercise the art and faculty of playing comedies, tragedies, histories, interludes, morals, pastorals, stage plays, and such others like as they have already studied or hereafter shall use or study, as well for the recreation of our loving subjects as for our solace and pleasure when we shall think good to see them during our pleasure.[66]

This license made the Lord Chamberlain's Men servants of the king and as such they changed the name of their company to the King's Men. The license also permitted the company to play where and when they wanted without having to put up with harassment from local officials. Gone were the days when actors could be whipped as "sturdy beggars."[67] As members of the royal household, each of the men named in the royal license received four and a half yards of scarlet-red cloth for his livery (a uniform worn by royal servants and retainers) and was expected to march in the royal procession, which, because of the plague, was postponed for a year until March 1604. The royal license testifies to the fact that Shakespeare and his company were the most important acting troupe in existence at that time.

The reign of James I not only endorsed the status of acting as a legitimate profession for Shakespeare and his fellow actors, but was profitable for them as well. Under James, the rate of pay for court performances was raised from the ten pounds Queen Elizabeth had paid to twenty pounds a performance. The number of performances at court was doubled because both King James and his wife, Queen Anne, were fascinated by English drama and

King James I (pictured) and his wife loved the theater, Shakespeare's acting company in particular.

could not get enough of it. They wanted to see all the plays they had missed living in Scotland. Shakespeare and his company were happy to oblige and performed more times at court than all the other London acting companies combined. Money flowed into the troupe's coffers. This was the most profitable time that the profession of acting had yet enjoyed.

In October 1603, Shakespeare demonstrated his skill for the new king. James I visited Lady Pembroke at Wilton House and witnessed a production of Shakespeare's *As You Like It*. The performance must have made a good impression because in December 1604 the players were asked to perform for the king again. This time they presented *Measure for Measure*, which Shakespeare had written the previous summer and which was calculated to appeal to James I because it dealt with issues close to the new king's heart: justice and mercy. Like the main character in the play, Duke Vincentio, James did not like crowds, and the character offered an idealized authority figure with whom the king could sympathize. *Measure for Measure* is Shakespeare's last comedy, and the ending of the play points to a dissatisfaction on Shakespeare's part with the conventional "happy ending" of comedies. Of the three marriages that conclude the play, two of them are spur of the moment and appear to have been injected by Shakespeare just so he would have a happy ending.

For a time, Shakespeare turned away from the genre of comedy to tragedy. In a tragedy "man loses, but during his doomed progress he discovers . . . the innermost recesses and finest discriminations of the human soul."[68] The tragedies that Shakespeare wrote not only live up to this idea but surpass it.

James I

No single historical event had a more direct impact on Shakespeare's livelihood than the death of Queen Elizabeth and the ascension of King James of Scotland to the throne of England. The production of some of Shakespeare's greatest plays can be traced to this era. The following passage from Samuel Schoenbaum's Shakespeare: The Globe and the World *describes King James's entry into London:*

"Of middle height, with broad shoulders and a thin, square beard, James had sandy hair, a nose too big for his face and a tongue too big for his puckered mouth. His skin bore a girlish softness, and his legs were so bent and spindly from a childhood bout with rickets that he required assistance when he walked. Not surprisingly, he preferred to ride. If James seemed corpulent, that was because he wore a thickly padded doublet to safeguard his royal body from would-be assassins' daggers. The new King reluctantly placed himself on view. In this respect, as in others, he differed from his predecessor. He 'did not caress the people nor make them that good cheer the late Queen did, whereby she won their loves,' observed the Venetian ambassador. James himself made the point less diplomatically. 'God's wounds!' he expostulated when notified his subjects wished to see him, 'I will pull down my breeches and they shall see my arse.' Had he done so, they would have glimpsed perhaps his best feature.

Expectant hordes thronged the capital for the coronation scheduled to take place that summer. 'The streets,' we hear, 'were plumed with gallants, tobacconists filled up whole taverns, vintners hung out spick-and-span new ivy bushes.' But once again pestilence gripped London, even more severely this time than in the previous decade. Each week more than eleven hundred were dying in the city and suburbs. Inevitably, the authorities barred the general public from the ceremonies at which, on July 25th, the first Stuart was crowned at Westminster. The royal progress through the streets, for which the municipal father had made elaborate preparations, was canceled; workmen took down the seven Arches of Triumph laboriously erected at great cost. The arches rose again the next year, however, after the plague had abated."

Written between 1603 and 1607, *Othello, King Lear, Macbeth,* and *Antony and Cleopatra* are considered to be Shakespeare's finest work. They are the work of a mature artist at the pinnacle of his creative power. One writer has said:

> Perhaps the most distinctive feature of Shakespeare's tragedies when compared to other great classics is the immediate accessibility of these masterpieces which, through their overwhelming humanity and imaginative range, have uniquely stood the test of time. . . . Interpretations of these works since their first performances at the Globe Theater . . . to the present day provide unique insights into the cultural history of the last four centuries.[69]

The power of these plays lies not in what is produced on the stage but what effect it produces in the mind of the viewer or reader.

Othello was the first play written during this period of Shakespeare's life, although it is not his first tragedy. Of all the tragedies, *Othello* is unique because of its focus on the unequal marriage between Othello, a Moorish (an African) mercenary, and Desdemona, the daughter of an aristocrat. Driven to jealousy by the accusations of Iago, who tells Othello that his wife is cheating on him, Othello kills his wife, and then realizing his mistake, kills himself. *Othello* is a dark play that explores the results of an unequal marriage and the mistake of placing too much faith in friends without questioning their motives. *Othello* is a key play in Shakespeare's dramatic development. It looks backward at the tragic figure of Hamlet and the romantic tragedy of *Romeo and Juliet* while at the same time looking forward to the even darker *Macbeth* and the romantic tragedy of *Antony and Cleopatra*.

Between the years 1603 and 1607, Shakespeare wrote some of his finest works, including Othello *and* King Lear.

If *Othello* reads like a romantic tragedy, then *King Lear* reads like a fairy tale. It begins with King Lear dividing his kingdom among his three daughters, two of whom are evil, while the youngest daughter, Cordelia, is good. Cordelia is, in fact, too good, and Lear disowns her because she refuses to flatter him and instead tells him the truth. Afterward, the two evil daughters, Goneril and Regan, gradually strip their father of everything he owns and then throw him out. As Lear wanders through a storm, he realizes the true meaning of kingship and the dreadful inadequacies of man-made justice. At least one critic has observed that "Lear recalls Othello in folly and in rage."[70] By the end of the play, everyone is dead.

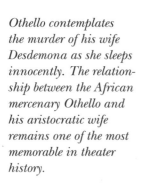

Othello contemplates the murder of his wife Desdemona as she sleeps innocently. The relationship between the African mercenary Othello and his aristocratic wife remains one of the most memorable in theater history.

King Lear provides no answers and no rewards. The good and the bad in it die alike and no tangible prospect is extended at the end of the play of a better future or of a Christian salvation beyond it. It is precisely this reason that for centuries the play was deemed both unacceptable and morally unsound.[71]

Because the death of the innocent Cordelia contradicts any sense of poetic justice, the play was rewritten by Nahum Tate in 1681 so that Cordelia lived and married the king of France. The play was performed that way until 1843 even though such an ending contradicted any sense of "real" life. *King Lear* is Shakespeare's most hopeless play. There is no room for happy endings, because "*King Lear* remains firmly rooted in the human, material world of the living and dying."[72]

If *King Lear* is Shakespeare's most hopeless play, then *Macbeth* is his darkest. In *Macbeth,* Shakespeare realizes the full potential of tragedy. It tells the story of a

righteous king murdered by his best general and kinsman, Macbeth, who then assumes the murdered king's throne. By the conclusion of the play, Macbeth has killed not only the king, but his comrade-in-arms Banquo, as well as women and children. One writer has said: "The play is about the growth and consequences of evil, and the violent disruption of natural order."[73] Another critic has said that *Macbeth* "is a short play, of intense concentration, like a dark and sinister opera."[74]

Macbeth is an unusual play because of the references Shakespeare makes to contemporary events. The play refers to the Gunpowder Plot of November 1605 when Catholic radicals packed the cellar of the Parliament building with gunpowder in an attempt to blow up King James I and all the members of Parliament. The plot was discovered at the last minute and the king and the members of Parliament were saved. Passages in the play also refer to the subsequent trial of the Catholic priest Henry Garnett in March 1606. Garnett was on trial because he knew about the plot, and although he disagreed with the plotters, he failed to tell anyone about it because he had learned of it through a confession. What was really on trial was the Jesuit philosophy of equivocation, a theme that runs throughout *Macbeth*. Equivocation means "the right and duty to keep a secret [like a secret told to a priest in confession], without telling a direct lie, by giving an answer that has two meanings and letting the questioner deceive himself."[75] Macbeth's downfall is brought about through the equivocation of the witches who tell him that "none of woman born" shall harm him (Macbeth is killed at the end of the play by Macduff who "was from his mother's womb / Untimely ripp'd"[76]).

Macbeth, like *Measure for Measure*, was calculated to appeal to King James. King James had an interest in witchcraft and had even written a book on demonology, so he was sure to have been pleased by the witches who play such a crucial role in the tragedy. The character of Banquo was also written to appeal to the king. James I traced his family lineage to a semimythical figure named Banquo. In the play, Macbeth is shown a vision by the witches in which it is made clear that, although Banquo will never be a king (he is murdered by Macbeth), his descendants will be kings. Macbeth remarks "What, will the line stretch out to th' crack of doom?"[77] The remark has proved prophetic because descendants of James I, members of the house Stuart, still control the throne of Britain today.

Antony and Cleopatra has been described as "the most exalted [tragedy], in the great sweep of its verse and a sense of nobility and of immortality attendant on love."[78] Like the earlier *Romeo and Juliet*, the play deals with the ill-fated love of two people from different backgrounds. While Romeo and Juliet are love-crazed teenagers who do not know any better, Antony and Cleopatra are both adults, both are leaders of their people and should know better. Although Antony and Romeo are similar in being swept up by the emotion of love into making irrational choices, Juliet and Cleopatra are nothing alike. Where Juliet is a shy virgin, Cleopatra "is unique among Shakespeare's women: immensely temperamental and dominating, using her sexual

Shakespeare wrote the witch scenes in Macbeth *especially to appeal to James I (pictured), who had an interest in witches and demonology.*

attraction to subjugate Antony; mercurial and variable; undependable, she lets her lover down; given up to pleasure and quite amoral, she is above all alien."[79] Some commentators have gone so far as to claim that Cleopatra is an elaboration of the Dark Lady of the sonnets. *Antony and Cleopatra* is a play about choices, right and wrong; it is also a play of fixity and flux, illustrating the conflict between passion (as embodied by Cleopatra and Egypt) and reason (as symbolized by Antony and Rome). Even though it is reason that ultimately wins out in the end, it is the tragic passion of *Antony and Cleopatra* that audiences remember and that has made their names immortal.

Noted Shakespearean scholar A. C. Bradley has defined tragedy as the story of "human actions producing exceptional calamity and ending in the death"[80] of the hero (or heroes). The themes of the tragedies "reach below the rational into the realm of the subconscious, into the primitive experiences which exist in the recesses of every human mind, though we may be unwilling to acknowledge them."[81] This idea accounts for the timeless nature of Shakespeare's tragedies: They are mirrors in which the human condition is reflected.

Coriolanus is a tragedy like *Antony and Cleopatra*, but where *Antony and Cleopatra* is "lush and romantic, *Coriolanus* is classical and stark, with a bitter taste." *Coriolanus* is

Michael Redgrave and Peggy Ashford star as Antony and Cleopatra in a 1953 production of the play held in Stratford-upon-Avon. The intense passion between Antony and Cleopatra, which ultimately leads to their undoing, has captivated audiences for centuries.

Shakespeare's most political play and reflects many of the issues current at the time. Peasants were being thrown off land at an increasing rate, and angry at losing the only life they knew, they began to riot in several towns and villages. Shakespeare, a landowner, was concerned about these rioting mobs; *Coriolanus* reflects his concern. In previous plays, Shakespeare "had treated the mob with contemptuous good humor; now his attitude has hardened"[82] into open hostility. *Coriolanus* contains Shakespeare's least sympathetic character and, as a result, is one of the public's least favorite plays.

The next play, *Timon of Athens,* is not a tragedy in the strictest sense of the word but a comedy of manners. It tells the story of a man who is surrounded by flatterers, and these flatterers give Timon gifts only because they know he will return to them more than was originally given.

> We learn that Timon's generosity is based upon a false estimate of his own nature, and of his followers. He is unaware that he is buying love and admiration. Deceived by appearance and false protestation, he fails to see that the principal motive of everybody, from the Senate down, is greed.[83]

Once Timon discovers the truth behind his friends' behavior, he becomes disgusted with society and retreats to a cave in the woods where he gives money to bandits and prostitutes so they can destroy society. Even though *Timon of Athens* is an unfinished play, it still provides a link to the "romance" plays he was to write toward the end of his career in which he successfully blends elements of both comedy and tragedy into a genre wholly of his own creation.

In 1608, Shakespeare became a one-seventh sharer in the Blackfriars Theatre. This was the same theater that was remodeled by James Burbage in 1597 but that the city authorities had prevented him from using. After the death of James Burbage, the theater passed into the possession of his sons, Richard and Cuthbert, who eventually ended up subleasing it to a boys' acting company called Children of the Chapel in 1600. The Children of the Chapel, and other groups like them, specialized in plays that satirized society and popular figures, and as a result, they got into trouble with the government authorities several times. These "boys' companies" were Shakespeare's primary competition, and he pokes fun at them in a couple of his plays. When the lease for the Children of the Chapel was up in 1608, the children moved out and Shakespeare and the King's Men moved in.

The Romance Plays

Because of the differences in seating and audience between the Globe and Blackfriars, Shakespeare was forced to produce a different kind of play. Blackfriars was an intimate theater, seating only three hundred people compared to the three thousand that might squeeze into the Globe on any given day. At the Globe, performances took place in the afternoon, usually starting around two o'clock and ending before sunset, whereas performances at Blackfriars usually took place in the evenings and were illuminated by candlelight. Because seating was limited, ticket prices were higher, and the audience was a little more select and sophisticated than the average

Globe audience. Eventually, the Blackfriars became more profitable than the Globe and Shakespeare's investment more than doubled its value. The success of the Blackfriars Theatre was at least partly due to the plays that Shakespeare wrote for this new select audience.

Shakespeare wrote neither tragedies, histories, nor romantic comedies but a curious blend of all three genres called a "romance." Typically, a romance told

> ancient (often Greek) stories of love as an overwhelming experience, inspiring amazing quests and vivid, usually incredible, encounters, and plots, intrigues, dangers (particularly from the elements and wild beasts), coincidences, disguises, conflicts of loyalty, losses and recoveries, births and deaths, and the eventual reunion of lovers, and parents and children. The characters are preferably of royal or noble birth, and happily lack much psychological plausibility in their actions.[84]

In 1608, Shakespeare wrote his first romance, *Pericles*. It is thought that *Pericles* was not originally written by Shakespeare but that he came across an older play and rewrote it for revival. *Pericles* tells of the adventures of Pericles who flees a murderous king, survives a shipwreck, wins his wife in a tournament only to lose her at sea, and then regains her and his grown daughter years later. Although the play is in no way realistic, it must have been spectacular within the intimate confines of the Blackfriars Theatre. The popularity of *Pericles* is attested to by the lively printing history it enjoyed before and after Shakespeare's death even though it was, in the words of Ben Jonson, a "mouldy tale."[85]

Cymbeline was a direct outgrowth of *Pericles* and contains the same plot devices common to all the romances (quests inspired by love, intrigues, coincidences, disguises, births, deaths, and the reunion of separated lovers). Like *Pericles, Cymbeline* was popular with audiences but not with critics, who tend to view it as "an uneven hollow hodgepodge."[86] However displeasing it was to critics, audiences loved it, and it seems to have pleased even courtly tastes, because the master of revels recorded that the play was performed on January 1, 1634, at court and that the king was pleased. Both *Cymbeline* and *Pericles* were popular with audiences for the same reason "action movies" are popular with modern audiences: special effects and happy endings. Both romances have gods who descend from the heavens to direct human affairs, ghosts, and villains, and both conclude with the reunion of families and separated lovers who have remained true to each other through it all.

A Successful Country Gentleman

These spectacles further increased Shakespeare's celebrity status. Indeed, Shakespeare's popularity had grown so much during the opening decade of the seventeenth century that his works were being openly pirated by booksellers and publishers. Since copyright laws (laws that protect an author's rights to his or her work) did not exist, publishers were free to print whatever manuscripts they could get their hands on and book merchants were free to sell what books were published, and nobody had to pay the author a thing. Theater companies jealously guarded their

Samuel Johnson's Evaluation of Shake[...]

As soon as Shakespeare died, people began to write about and discuss his works and their impact on English-speaking society. In this essay reprinted from The Norton Anthology of English Literature, *Samuel Johnson examines the reasons behind Shakespeare's enduring popularity.*

"Shakespeare is, above all writers, [...] modern writers, the poet of nature, [...] up to his readers a faithful mirror [...] life. His characters are not modifie[...] particular places, unpracticed by th[...] by the peculiarities of studies or professions, which can operate but upon small numbers; or by the accidents of transient fashions or temporary opinions: they are the genuine progeny of common humanity, such as the world will always supply and observation will always find. His persons act and speak by the influence of those general passions and principles by which all minds are agitated and the whole system of life is continued in motion. In the writings of other poets a character is too often an individual; in those of Shakespeare it is commonly a species.

It is this which fills the plays of Shakespeare with practical axioms and domestic wisdom. It was said of Euripides that every verse was a precept; and it may be said of Shakespeare that from his works may be collected a system of civil and economical prudence. Yet his real power is not shown in the splendor of particular passages, but by the progress of his fable and the tenor of his dialogue. . . .

Shakespeare has no heroes; his scenes are occupied only by men, who act and speak as the reader thinks that he should himself have spoken or acted on the same occasion. . . .

This therefore is the praise of Shakespeare, that his drama is the mirror of life; that he who has mazed his imagination in following the phantoms which other writers raise up before him, may here be cured of his delirious ecstasies by reading human sentiments in human language, by scenes from which a hermit may estimate the transactions of the world, and a confessor predict the progress of the passions."

playbooks becaus[...]
published, us[...]
lated version[...]
it. Dema[...]
Shakes[...]
high[...]

...e once a play was openly ...ally in a hopelessly muti... ..., any company could perform ...d for these pirated versions of ...eare's plays (called quartos) was ..., and many of his plays were published ...ring his lifetime without his permission. It is under these conditions that Shakespeare's greatest piece of nondramatic poetry was published.

In 1609, a slim volume of poems titled Shakespeare's *Sonnets* appeared in the stalls of booksellers around London. The book was prefaced with this mysterious dedication:

> TO.THE.ONLY.BEGETTER.OF.
> THESE.ENSUING.SONNETS.
> Mr.W.H. ALL.HAPPINESS.
> AND.THAT.ETERNITY.
> PROMISED.
> BY.
> OUR.EVER-LIVING.POET.
> WISHETH.
> THE.WELL-WISHING.
> ADVENTURER.IN.
> SETTING.
> FORTH.
> T.T.

As can be seen, the dedication was written not by the author of the sonnets (as was customary) but by the publisher of the poems, a mysterious figure by the name of Thomas Thorpe. This, and the fact that the edition was riddled with mistakes, has led scholars to conclude that Shakespeare had no hand in the publication and that Thorpe got the manuscript from some other source, most likely the enigmatic "Mr. W. H." of the dedication. The identity of Mr. W. H. has been widely guessed at but as of this date, no answer has been universally accepted. The wording and punc-

tuation of the dedication appear to have been deliberately constructed in such a way as to hide Mr. W. H.'s identity. Regardless of the circumstances surrounding the publication of Shakespeare's sonnets, they remain some of the most popular poems of all time.

Shakespeare's good fortune was not restricted to his professional life but was also rolling over into his private life as well. Because of his financial success in the theater, Shakespeare was able to buy a half-

The title page for the 1609 edition of the sonnets that historians suspect Shakespeare had no hand in because of the numerous mistakes found in the volume.

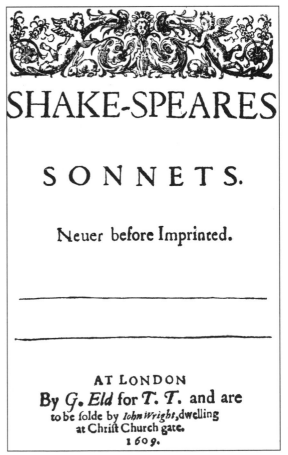

SHAKE-SPEARES

SONNETS.

Neuer before Imprinted.

AT LONDON
By *G. Eld* for *T. T.* and are
to be folde by *Iohn Wright,* dwelling
at Chrift Church gate.
1609.

Renaissance Printing Practices

The following passage from The Shakespeare Handbook *discusses Elizabethan printing practices:*

"At this period, copyright laws only existed as a legal instrument used by the government for the purposes of censorship. It did not rest with the author but with the stationer, publisher, or printer who registered the book's title with the Stationer's Company and gained the license to print it. Generally dramatists and the acting companies for which they wrote were loath to see their plays in print. A complete play script was a unique document and represented a capital asset to a company for as long as it was popular with the theater-going public. Once published, it would generate money for the publisher or, worse, could be performed by a rival company, both resulting in a likely loss of revenue. The King's Men won an injunction in 1619 preventing the printing of their plays without permission, but even this was circumvented by the printer and bookseller William Jaggard and the publisher Thomas Pavier who were already halfway through production of a collection of nine Shakespearean and pseudo-Shakespearean reprints. They issued the five remaining titles, including *A Midsummer Night's Dream, The Merchant of Venice,* and *King Lear,* with title pages falsely dated 1600 and 1608."

interest in tithes in Old Stratford in 1605. A half-interest in tithes assured Shakespeare of not only a steady profit off his investment but also a steady supply of produce and grains. Shakespeare was becoming one of the richest men in Stratford.

In 1607, Shakespeare's oldest daughter, Susanna, married Dr. John Hall. Then, as now, a marriage to a doctor was a prestigious and desirable match. One year later, in 1608, Susanna gave birth to Shakespeare's first granddaughter, Elizabeth Hall. Later that same year, Shakespeare's mother, Mary, died. She was buried next to her husband in the churchyard at Stratford-upon-Avon, where she had spent the biggest part of her life.

During this period, Shakespeare was involved in a couple of lawsuits whose records are more numerous than interesting. In 1604, Shakespeare sold his Stratford neighbor Phillip Rogers twenty bushels of malt and lent him two shillings. Later that year, Shakespeare had to file suit against his neighbor in order to recover the debt. It is not known how, or if, the court ruled on the matter. A few years later in 1608, Shakespeare again filed suit against another neighbor, John Addenbrooke, who owed the poet six pounds. The lawsuit dragged on for more than a year until the court decided in Shakespeare's favor and ordered Addenbrooke to pay what was owed. The court records do not tell if the debt was ever collected. Shakespeare's persistence in these matters may strike some people as heartless, but it must be remembered that Shakespeare was primarily a businessman, and in an age without credit cards or collection agencies, suing in court was the only way to recover a debt. The most important thing these records tell us is that as of 1608 or 1609 Shakespeare had moved back to Stratford and had become a permanent resident who made infrequent trips to London to see to his theater business and to produce an occasional play. Shakespeare was settling into the role of the successful country gentleman.

6 Back to Stratford

Nicholas Rowe, an early biographer, has summed up Shakespeare's later years:

> The latter part of his life was spent, as all men of good sense will wish theirs may be, in ease, retirement, and the conversation of his friends. He had the good fortune to gather an estate equal to his occasion, and, in that, to his wish; and is said to have spent some years before his death at his native Stratford.[87]

After turning his back on the city that made him famous, "William Shakespeare of Stratford-upon-Avon in the county of Warwick, gentleman"[88] settled into New Place and began to take a more active interest in the affairs of his hometown.

In 1611, Shakespeare was involved, along with several other people, in a lawsuit to defend his Stratford tithes in the Court of Chancery. It is unknown what the result of the lawsuit was, but Shakespeare continued to collect profits from the holdings until his death in 1616. This is not the only time that Shakespeare went to court to defend his investments because a few years later, in 1614, Shakespeare was again in court fighting the enclosure of certain lands in Welcombe that would have adversely affected his tithes. Shakespeare also signed his name to a petition that was sent to Parliament to ask for financial assistance with improving the road from Stratford to London. Since Shakespeare made the trip from Stratford to London at least once a year, he had a vested interest in seeing the road improved. However, like many bills of its kind written by the common people to Parliament, the ruling class ignored it and, subsequently, nothing came of it.

During this period, Shakespeare not only sued and was sued, he was also called as a witness in a sticky lawsuit concerning an arranged marriage. In 1604, Shakespeare was renting a room from a Mr. and Mrs. Mountjoy (all the years he lived in London, Shakespeare never purchased a home of his own but rented rooms near the theaters where he worked), and while he was living there, he was called upon by Mr. and Mrs. Mountjoy to help negotiate a marriage agreement for their daughter Mary to their apprentice Stephen Belott, who was holding out for a better dowry. Shakespeare negotiated an agreement that seemed beneficial to both sides and the wedding took place on November 19, 1604, in the church of St. Olave in Silver Street near the Mountjoys' home.

Soon after the marriage, things began to fall apart. Instead of staying on in Mountjoy's shop to help, as the father had expected, the newlyweds moved out and set

up their own shop. Angry about the perceived betrayal, Mountjoy gave the couple
ten pounds and some old household
stuff—some old furniture and a bed, some
worn blankets, coarse napkins, and two
scissors—instead of the promised dowry.
In 1606, Mrs. Mountjoy died and the Be-
lotts moved back in with Mr. Mountjoy
to help with the shop. Arguments over
money followed and the couple packed up
and moved out once again. The final straw
was a rumor that Mr. Mountjoy intended
to cut off his daughter and her husband in
his will. Hence the lawsuit.

It was the court's job to decide what, if
any, financial obligation existed at the time
of the marriage. Since Shakespeare had
helped to arrange the marriage, in 1612
he was called upon to testify to the terms
of the marriage as he remembered them;
both sides in the lawsuit looked forward to
his testimony. However, because of his age
(he was nearly forty-eight years old, old for
the time) or because he had no personal
stake in the matter, he could not remember the details of the agreement. The
court referred the matter for arbitration to
the elders of the local church, who decided that both men were equally at fault
but awarded Belott twenty nobles anyway.
A year later, Mountjoy still had not paid
the sum. The Belott-Mountjoy lawsuit is interesting because it offers a glimpse into
Shakespeare's world and shows him living
amid the raw material for a romantic comedy like *The Merry Wives of Windsor* or *The
Taming of the Shrew.*

William Shakespeare was busy in 1613.
In the previous year, Shakespeare's younger brother Gilbert died at the age of forty-
six; he was buried on February 3. The
death was quite a blow to Shakespeare because this was the brother he was closest to

*William Shakespeare spent his elder years in rel-
ative leisure, enjoying life on his country estate,
New Place.*

and upon whom he had depended to take
care of his business in Stratford while he
had been away in London tending to his
theater business. Exactly a year and a day
later, Shakespeare's other brother, Richard,
died and was buried on February 4, 1613.
Of the eight sons and daughters that John
and Mary Shakespeare had brought into
the world, only two now survived: the poet
and his sister Joan, who would outlive
William by thirty years. With the majority
of his siblings dead, William Shakespeare
knew that his end was fast approaching,
but he did not let up on the pace of the
work he was doing.

There was no time for grief because
that same February Shakespeare and the
King's Men were called upon to provide

entertainment for the wedding celebrations marking the marriage of King James's daughter, Princess Elizabeth, to Prince Frederick, the Elector Palatine of the Rhine. The King's Men entertained the royal newlyweds and their guests with no fewer than fourteen plays, performing *Much Ado About Nothing, Othello, The Winter's Tale,* and *The Tempest* among others. For their trouble, the acting troupe was paid a little more than ninety-three pounds. By way of comparison, Lady Elizabeth's Men, the princess's own actors, played only twice during the celebration, which testifies to the preeminence of Shakespeare's acting company in London at this time.

Enjoying Semiretirement

In March 1613, Shakespeare made his last investment in property, but this time not in Stratford. Instead, he bought half the gatehouse of the old Blackfriars monastery in London. The reason for this purchase has more to do with convenience than with profit. The gatehouse was ideally located, so Shakespeare would have easy access to the theaters where his plays were produced. The indoor theater in the Blackfriars monastery was just across the courtyard from the gatehouse, and at the end of the street was Puddle Dock where Shakespeare could catch a water taxi across the Thames River to Bankside and the Globe Theatre.

Later that same month, on March 31, 1613, Shakespeare and Richard Burbage were each paid forty-four shillings for supplying an "impresa" for Lord Rutland. An impresa is an "insignia, allegorical or mythological, with appropriate mottoes . . .

painted on paper shields." [89] The impresa was made for the ceremonies surrounding the anniversary of King James's accession to the throne of England. The impresa must not have been that noteworthy because a witness to the anniversary festivities reports that some of the impresa "were so dark, that their meaning is not yet understood, unless perchance that were their meaning, not to be understood." [90]

On June 29, 1613, the Globe burned to the ground during a performance of Shakespeare's latest play, *Henry VIII.* Sir Henry Wotton, who was not present at the time of the fire, describes what happened in a letter to his nephew Sir Edmund Bacon:

> Now, King Henry making a masque at the Cardinal Wolsey's house, and certain chambers [cannons] being shot off at his entry, some of the paper, or other stuff, wherewith one of them [the cannon] was stopped, did light on the thatch, where being thought at first but idle smoke, and their eyes more attentive to the show, it kindled inwardly, and ran round like a train, consuming within less than an hour the whole house to the very grounds. This was the fatal period of that virtuous fabric, wherein yet nothing did perish but wood and straw, and a few forsaken cloaks; only one man had his breeches set on fire that would have broiled him, if he had not the benefit of a provident wit put it out with bottle ale. [91]

The fact that nobody was killed during the fire is miraculous considering that the Globe held close to three thousand people and had only one entrance that also doubled as an exit. The fire also inspired several people to write satirical poems about the event. The city authorities and religious leaders saw the hand of God at work in the fire and were glad that the public nuisance was no more. Their happiness was short-lived because within a year the Globe had been reconstructed and was again open for business.

Shakespeare was extremely busy during these years producing plays for the public and the court, not to mention handling his business affairs in both London and Stratford, but he still managed to write. For most of his career, Shakespeare wrote about two plays a year, but after moving back to Stratford, this dropped to about one a year. The reason for this has to do with his enjoying himself in semiretirement rather than being bored with drama

Shakespeare's Language

One of the most frequent complaints modern readers make about Shakespeare's plays is the difficulty of the language. This is not a new problem. In 1679, sixty-three years after Shakespeare's death in 1616, the poet John Dryden complained about the archaic nature of Shakespeare's language. This passage is from The Riverside Shakespeare.

"Yet it must be allow'd to the present Age that the tongue in general is so much refin'd since Shakespeare's time, that many of his words, and more of his Phrases, are scarce intelligible. And of those which we understand some are ungrammatical, others, course [coarse]; and his whole stile is so pester'd with Figurative expressions, that it is as affected as it is obscure. . . .

I cannot deny that he has his failings: but they are not so much in the passions themselves, as in his manner of expression: he often obscures his meaning by his words, and sometimes makes it unintelligible. I will not say of so great a Poet, that he distinguish'd not the blown puffy stile, from true sublimity; but I may venture to maintain that the fury of his fancy often transported him, beyond the bounds of Judgement, either in coyning of new words, and phrases, or racking words which were in use. . . .

If Shakespeare were stript of all the bombast in his passions, and dress'd in the most vulgar words, we should find the beauties of his thoughts remaining; if his embroideries were burnt down, there would still be the silver at the bottom of the melting-pot: but I fear (at least, let me fear it for my self) that we who Ape his sounding words, have nothing of his thought, but are all out-side; there is not so much as a dwarf within our Giant's cloaths."

or burned-out. The plays Shakespeare wrote during this period continued to be romances. The romances allowed Shakespeare to spread his dramatic and poetic wings in ways that the other genres could not, and they contain some of the finest dramatic poetry ever written in English.

The Winter's Tale was written during this latter period of Shakespeare's life, and like the previous romances, *Pericles* and *Cymbeline,* it was popular with audiences but attacked by critics. Its loose construction and impossibilities of plot have caused critics to say that Shakespeare "was hurried, negligent, or bored, worn out perhaps by writing all those histories and tragedies." However, the critical problems disappear if the play is taken at face value, that is, it is a "winter's tale" and was "not supposed to have credibility, consistency, or conciseness" [92] but was merely meant to entertain and to help pass the long winter nights. Writing *The Winter's Tale* gave Shakespeare some measure of personal satisfaction because the first three acts are a dramatization of Robert Greene's novel *Pandosto,* which claimed to be a cautionary tale about the evils of jealousy. Robert Greene, it will be remembered, was Shakespeare's first critic when he arrived on the London dramatic scene and called Shakespeare "an upstart crow, beautified with our feathers." [93] Not only does Shakespeare take Greene's "feathers" but he makes them more beautiful than Greene ever could.

After *The Winter's Tale,* Shakespeare wrote his most popular romance, *The Tempest,* which many critics see as his "farewell" play. *The Tempest* is, in Shakespeare's own words, "something rich and strange" [94] and contains more songs and music than any other play Shakespeare wrote. "*The Tempest* is primarily a play for the theater. It has a

This memorial bust of William Shakespeare is believed to be one of the few accurate likenesses of him. It is located in Holy Trinity Church, Stratford-upon-Avon, where the playwright is buried.

spectacular storm scene at the beginning, scenes of magical manipulation of people and things, a masque of goddesses, spirits in the form of a pack of hounds, a half-domesticated monster, and characters who can go about invisible to other characters." [95] It is Shakespeare's most theatrical play and contains many references to acting and the theater, as can be seen in a speech that the main character, Prospero, gives near the end of the play:

> Our revels now are ended. These
>   our actors
> (As I foretold you) were all spirits,
>   and,
> Are melted into air, into thin air,

The famed English actor John Gielgud as Prospero in a production of The Tempest. *The play is one of Shakespeare's most popular, and, many critics argue, his best written.*

And like the baseless fabric of this
    vision,
The cloud-capp'd tow'rs, the
    gorgeous palaces,
The solemn temples, the great
    globe itself,
Yea, all which it inherit, shall dissolve,
Leave not a rack behind. We are such
    stuff
As dreams are made on; and our
    little life
Is rounded with a sleep.[96]

The Tempest, along with *Hamlet,* is one of the most quoted plays Shakespeare wrote, although it is rarely performed be-cause of the technical demands that it makes upon the stage. Shakespeare uses dreams and references to the theater to illustrate one of the major themes of the play: the difference between reality and illusion. Everyone in the play is manipulated to some extent by Prospero's magic so that they cannot tell the difference between what is real and what is fantasy. This leads to another of the play's themes: servitude and freedom.

The Tempest is a remarkable play and is a favorite of both critics and audiences alike because of its fairy tale quality and the beauty of its poetry. The play ends with Prospero giving up his magic:

Graves at my command
Have wak'd their sleepers, op'd, and
    let 'em forth
By my so potent art. But this rough
    magic
I here abjure; and when I have
    requir'd
Some heavenly music (which even
    now I do)
To work mine end upon their senses
    that
This airy charm is for, I'll break my
    staff,
Bury it certain fadoms in the earth,
And deeper than did ever plummet
    sound
I'll drown my book.[97]

Many Shakespearean scholars have been tempted to see Prospero as Shakespeare and to view this speech as Shakespeare's farewell to the stage and playwriting. The idea has sentimental appeal and is only half accurate. After *The Tempest,* Shakespeare would collaborate on at least two more plays before his death. *The Tempest*—"this miraculous drama"[98] as Samuel Coleridge called it—has been a favorite of both audiences and readers and has inspired such vastly different writers as John Milton, T. S. Eliot, and W. H. Auden.

If *The Tempest* is the play that Shakespeare used to cap his progression of comedies and tragedies, then *Henry VIII* is the play that concluded the cycle of histories that had been started twenty-three years earlier. Now that Queen Elizabeth was dead, it was safe to explore the rule of her father, Henry VIII, who exerted a strong influence on the future of English history. To make this point clear, the focus of the play is not so much on individual charac-

ters or events but on the larger force of history to which all men are subject. Ultimately, the play

> is interested . . . in the discovery of historical and ethical truth. . . . But although *King Henry VIII* questions the existence of truth and the possibility of knowing it, philosophical scepticism is . . . transformed into visionary romance. . . . History now ceases to be

Shakespeare returned to history in his later years to write Henry VIII *(pictured). Scholars think that Shakespeare was not the sole author of the play.*

a dark enigma and becomes a process of ripening and fulfillment . . . [an] image of a life endlessly and inexhaustibly renewed.[99]

Henry VIII is interesting for another reason: Because of the textual inconsistencies, it is believed that Shakespeare was not the sole author but collaborated with John Fletcher to write it. Shakespeare is thought to have written the first half and then handed it to his young contemporary John Fletcher to finish. This is used to explain the awkwardness of the last half of the play. Little is known of Fletcher except that he often collaborated with a man by the name of Francis Beaumont as well as writing plays by himself and with other authors, such as

English dramatist and author John Fletcher (pictured) is believed to have collaborated with Shakespeare in the writing of Henry VIII. *After Shakespeare's death, Fletcher was considered the greatest playwright of the early seventeenth century.*

Shakespeare. Fletcher was closely associated with the King's Men and helped develop the new genre of romance (or as he called it, "tragicomedy"). After Shakespeare's death, during the late seventeenth century, Fletcher was considered the best playwright of the early part of the century, ranking even above Shakespeare. *Henry VIII* marks the beginning of a writing partnership between William Shakespeare and John Fletcher that was to last for three plays.

The second of these three plays, *Cardenio,* has been lost, but the third, *The Two Noble Kinsmen,* survives. Until recently, the play was not included in the collected works of Shakespeare, but since it has been determined that *Henry VIII* was written by Shakespeare and Fletcher and it has been included in the collected works, *The Two Noble Kinsmen* has been added to the canon. *The Two Noble Kinsmen* is a dramatization of "The Knight's Tale" by the early English poet Geoffrey Chaucer. The play explores the conflict between innocence and experience, between sexual desire and duty. It contains many of the elements of Shakespeare's romances but leans heavily upon the use of rhetoric and spectacle in order to make up for the lack of a plot and the uneven quality of the poetry, usually blamed not on Shakespeare but on his collaborator, Fletcher.

After working with Fletcher on *The Two Noble Kinsmen* in 1613, Shakespeare went into full-time retirement. He wrote no further works after 1613 as far as scholars can tell. Biographers have failed to turn up any records on him after the marginal role he played in a lawsuit to oppose the enclosure of lands he leased and received tithes from in 1614. It is a bit of harmless speculation to picture Shakespeare in his last years living at New Place in Stratford, the "local boy done well" home to enjoy the fruits of his quarter century in the theater business and to get to know the family he had hardly seen. Traveling to London once or twice a year to collect his share of the profits from the Globe and the Blackfriars Theatres, he was sure to have seen his old friends Richard Burbage and Ben Jonson. But it is speculation; nothing is known for sure about him until 1616.

The Death of Shakespeare

On February 10, 1616, Shakespeare's youngest daughter, Judith, married Thomas Quiney, the son of an old family friend. The marriage was unusual because the groom, a twenty-seven-year-old vintner with a reputation for shadiness, was marrying the thirty-one-year-old daughter of the most famous man, and one of the richest, in town. One gets the idea that Judith did not have much choice in mates since at thirty-one she was quickly becoming the town's old maid. In any case, the honeymoon was short-lived because after their marriage the Quineys were excommunicated for failing to obtain a special license for marriage during Lent, when marriages were normally forbidden. The excommunication lasted only a year, because the Quineys were back in church in 1617 to have their firstborn son, Shaksper Quiney, baptized.

However, in March 1616, the newly wed Thomas Quiney had bigger problems than excommunication. On the twenty-sixth of March, Quiney was summoned before the "bawdy court" for fornication. Before his marriage to Judith Shakespeare, Thomas Quiney had impregnated a woman by the name of Margaret Wheeler. By February, when Quiney married Judith Shakespeare, Margaret was "dangerously pregnant."[100] Scandal became tragedy a month after the wedding when Margaret Wheeler and her child died during childbirth. Thomas Quiney was made to appear before the "bawdy court," where he promptly confessed and threw himself on the mercy of the court. The judge in the case, John Rogers, sentenced Quiney to perform penance in a white sheet in the church on three successive Sundays before the whole congregation. Quiney was spared the public humiliation and the penalty was lowered to five shillings, which he was to give for the poor of the parish.

What began in February as a joyous time in William Shakespeare's life turned to embarrassment that spring of 1616, then to illness, and then, finally, to death. Perhaps the shock of having the "gentle" family name of Shakespeare associated with such a public scandal was too much for the fifty-one-year-old man. Or maybe it was coincidence that the inevitable would occur at this point in time. Whatever the reason, that March William Shakespeare became seriously ill.

The circumstances surrounding William Shakespeare's month-long illness and eventual death are unclear. One story has Shakespeare meeting with his friend Ben Jonson and his fellow Warwickshire-man Michael Drayton for a drinking party to celebrate his youngest daughter's marriage with the result that "Shakespear died of a fever there contracted."[101] It is conceivable that his son-in-law, Dr. Hall, treated him while he was ill, but Dr. Hall left no such record in his casebooks, which only date back as far as 1617, the year after Shakespeare's death.

The death mask of William Shakespeare. The playwright died on April 23, 1616.

The January before Judith's marriage, Shakespeare called upon lawyer Francis Collins to draw up and execute his last will and testament. After Judith's marriage, revisions to the document were necessary, so Collins was called upon again to make the revisions. It is because of his signature on these revisions (experts in handwriting say that these signatures are markedly different from other known Shakespeare signatures) that scholars and biographers have come to the conclusion that he was ill and dying, although he would linger for another month. Shakespeare's life came to a close on April 23, 1616, on St. George's Day, feast day of England's patron saint and, appropriately enough, the poet's fifty-second birthday. Two days later, the Stratford register records the burial of "Will Shakespere, gent."[102]

Shakespeare's will has stirred as much commentary as any of his plays. The Stratford historian Joseph Greene, who turned up a copy in 1747, was disappointed with his discovery:

The Legacies and Bequests therein . . . are undoubtedly as he intended; but the manner of introducing them, appears to me so dull and irregular, so absolutely void of [the] least particle of that Spirit which Animated Our great Poet; that it must lessen his character as a Writer to imagine [the] least Sentence of it his production.[103]

However, B. Roland Lewis, a twentieth-century student of Shakespeare, has a different view, writing: "Rowe [an early Shakespeare biographer] said that the spirit of the man [Shakespeare] is to be found in his works. Rather the essential spirit of William Shakespeare is to be found in his will, its preparation constituting virtually the last act of his active life only a few weeks before he died."[104]

Shakespeare's will is an interesting document for a few reasons. Shakespeare's arrangements for his youngest daughter, Judith, are odd. He provides her with a generous sum on the condition that her husband, Thomas Quiney, cannot touch it unless he can provide her with lands of equal value. The fact that Shakespeare has effectively cut off Quiney from any proceeds of his estate points to a resentment, or a distrust, of Quiney. Some people believe that the shock of the public scandal involving Quiney quickened Shakespeare's demise.

Lesser bequests follow. He leaves money to buy memorial rings for his countrymen, friends, and fellow actors to remember him by. He donates money to the poor of Stratford, and gives each of his sisters' sons five pounds. Shakespeare leaves the biggest part of his estate to his oldest daughter, Susanna, and her husband, Dr. John Hall. He leaves her New Place

and two messuages or tenements with the appurtences situate . . . in Henley

In Defense of Shakespeare

In the following excerpt from his "Essay of Dramatick Poesie" (as quoted in The Riverside Shakespeare*), poet John Dryden discusses Shakespeare's lack of education and compares him to Ben Jonson and other contemporary poets:*

"To begin then with Shakespeare; he was the man who of all Modern, and perhaps Ancient Poets, had the largest and most comprehensive soul. All the images of Nature were still present to him, and he drew them not laboriously, but luckily: when he describes any thing, you more than see it, you feel it too. Those who accuse him of having wanted learning, give him the greater commendation: he was naturally learn'd; he needed not the spectacles of books to read Nature; he look'd in wards, and found her there. I cannot say he is every where alike; were he so, I should do him injury to compare him with the greatest of Mankind. He is many times flat, insipid; his Comick wit degenerating into clenches, his serious swelling into Bombast. But he is always great, when some great occasion is presented to him: no man can say he ever had a fit subject for his wit, and did not then raise himself as high above the rest of the Poets. . . .

The consideration of this made Mr. Hales of Eaton say, that there was no subject of which any Poet ever writ, but he would produce it much better treated of in Shakespeare; and however others are now generally prefer'd before him, yet the Age wherein he liv'd, which had contemporaries with him, Fletcher and Jonson, never equall'd them to him in their esteem: And in the last Kings Court, when Ben's reputation was at highest, Sir John Suckling, and with him the greatest part of the Courtiers, set our Shakespeare far above him."

Street within the borough of Stratford aforesaid; and all my barns, stables, orchards, gardens, lands, tenements, and hereditaments whatsoever, situate . . . within the towns, hamlets, villages, fields, and grounds of Stratford upon Avon, Old Stratford, Bushupton, and Welcombe, or in any of them, in the said county of Warwick; and also all that messuage or tenement with the appurtenances wherein one John Robinson dwelleth, situate . . . in the Blackfriars in London, near the Wardrobe; and all other my lands, tenements, and hereditaments whatsoever.[105]

Then, on the last page of his will, Shakespeare remembers his wife, Anne: "Item. I give unto my wife my second best bed with the furniture."[106] This single item has generated as much comment as anything he ever wrote for the stage. Some people take it as a last slap at his wife and point out that he fails to provide for her in any other part of the will. Others argue that Shakespeare knew that Susanna and her husband were good people and that they would care for his wife after his death, which is why he left them more than anyone else. They also say that the best bed would be considered an heirloom and could be better used by the young couple, Susanna and Dr. Hall, and that the "second best bed" was probably the actual marriage bed he had shared with his wife. To support these assertions they point to similar provisions in other wills of the time period.[107]

Stratford's most illustrious citizen was laid to rest in the chancel (bone-house) of Holy Trinity Church in Stratford-upon-Avon. On the slab of stone that covers the poet's grave appears his epitaph, reportedly written by himself:

> GOOD FRIEND FOR JESUS SAKE
>   FORBEAR
> TO DIG THE DUST ENCLOSED
>   HERE:
> BLEST BE THE MAN THAT SPARES
>   THESE STONES,
> AND CURST BE HE THAT MOVES
>   MY BONES.[108]

The stone that covers the poet's grave in Holy Trinity Church. Most critics believe that Shakespeare wrote the epitaph himself.

The words are not directed at the pilgrim come to pay homage or to the casual passerby but to the sexton, or caretaker of the church. Because of the limited space available for burial, the sexton would sometimes dig up graves and place the old bones in a common burial chamber to make room for a new corpse. The curse seems to have worked because no sexton or graverobber has ever disturbed Shakespeare's bones. Seven years later, when his wife, Anne, died, she requested that the grave be opened so that she could be laid to rest next to the husband who had spent so much time away from her. Citing the curse, the sexton flatly refused and she was buried in a separate grave to the right of her husband on August 8, 1623.

As soon as Shakespeare had been laid in his grave, Stratford began to receive a steady stream of pilgrims that came to pay their respects to the greatest playwright of the English language. So that they would not be disappointed by the plain stone that covers his grave, Shakespeare's family joined his friends from the theater and in 1623 erected a monument to him in Holy Trinity Church. The monument contains a bust of Shakespeare and the following epitaph:

> IVDICIO PYLIUM, GENIO
>   SOCRATEM, ARTE MARONEM,
> TERRA TEGIT, POPULUS MAERET,
>   OLYMPUS HABET
> [In judgment a Nestor, in wit a
>   Socrates, in art a Virgil; the earth
>   buries him, the people mourn
>   him, Olympus possesses him]
> STAY PASSENGER, WHY GOEST
>   THOU BY SO FAST?
> READ IF THOU CANST, WHOM
>   ENVIOUS DEATH HATH PLAST,
> WITH IN THIS MONUMENT
>   SHAKESPEARE: WITH WHOM
> QUICK NATURE DIED: WHOSE
>   NAME DOTH DECK THE TOMB,
> FAR MORE THEN COST: SINCE
>   ALL THAT HE HATH WRIT,
> LEAVES LIVING ART, BUT PAGE,
>   TO SERVE HIS WIT. [109]

7 Shakespeare Today

The story of William Shakespeare does not end with his death but only begins. During his life, Shakespeare published nothing himself except for three poems ("Venus and Adonis," "The Rape of Lucrece," and "The Phoenix and the Turtle"). The reason for not publishing was financial: Copyright laws as known today did not exist so if the plays were published, anyone could perform them and profit from them.

If it had not been for two of William Shakespeare's theater friends, John Heminge and Henry Condell, his plays would not exist today. After Shakespeare's death, they took upon themselves the difficult task of assembling all the play manuscripts into a single publication that has come to be known as the First Folio, or the Folio of 1623. It is because of this book that the majority of Shakespeare's plays have been preserved while all of his personal papers, manuscripts, and books have disappeared. The First Folio was unusual because the only other writer to ever collect all his writings into one book was Shakespeare's friendly rival, Ben Jonson, who issued his collected *Works* early in 1623.

The First Folio, published in November 1623, contained all of Shakespeare's plays as known today except for *Pericles* and *The Two Noble Kinsmen.* (It is thought they were excluded because they were collabo-rations between Shakespeare and Fletcher.) It contained a flawed portrait of Shake-speare by Martin Droeshout, a dedication to the patrons of the King's Men, William, who was the earl of Pembroke and the Lord Chamberlain, and his brother Philip, earl of Montgomery. It was prefaced with a prologue by Heminge and Condell that asked the reader to "Judge your sixe-pen'orth, your shillings worth, your five shillings worth at a time, or higher, so you rise to the just rates, and welcome. But whatever you do, buy,"[110] because the book was expensive to produce and they were not sure it would sell. The First Folio con-tained memorial poems to Shakespeare by Ben Jonson, Hugh Holland, and Leonard Digges. Although Shakespeare's wife, Anne, lived to see the memorial installed in Strat-ford's Holy Trinity Church, she died be-fore the First Folio was printed. The First Folio was such a success that it was reprinted four times by 1685, and since that time, Shakespeare's plays have been reprinted thousands, perhaps millions, of times and have been translated into all the major languages of the world.

William Shakespeare's biggest impact has been on the English language. No other writer in the English language has coined so many words and phrases that are still in use today. Some of the words are no longer commonly used, such as *kickshaw* (the serving of fancy food; trinket or trifle). But many of them are still in use: *Anchovy, assassination, bump, frugal, invulnerable, lonely, mountaineer, quarrelsome, skim milk, yelping,* and *zany* are words coined by Shakespeare.

Shakespeare's plays have become such a part of Western society that he is often quoted without the speaker knowing it. If you have ever described something as "without rhyme or reason," or called someone an "eyesore" or a "laughingstock," or "laughed yourself into stitches," you are quoting Shakespeare. He likewise coined the phrases "tongue-tied," "as dead as a doornail," "give the devil his due," "green-eyed jealousy," and "melted into thin air," just to name a few from a list that could go on for pages.

William Shakespeare not only contributed to the English language but is also responsible for drama as it is known today. Before Shakespeare, acting was a disreputable profession and actors could, and were, whipped as "Rogues, Vagabonds, and Sturdy Beggars." [111] It is because of Shakespeare's success, both as a businessman and as a writer, that theater today has such a high position in the realm of the dramatic arts. Shakespeare almost singlehandedly turned acting from the occupation of "Rogues, Vagabonds, and Sturdy Beggars" into a gentlemanly profession that was supported and acclaimed by both the upper and the lower classes, from the king to the peasants.

Shakespeare is also responsible for the play as it is known today. Before Shakespeare, drama was written within the confines of what was known as the classical unities: "Unity of Time (the stage action to last a few hours, as long as the performance); Place (everything to happen in one location); and Action (no subplots)." [112] Shakespeare broke this tradition and allowed the time of his plays to span years and the action to shift between locations as varied as England and Italy, Sicily and Bohemia. His plays are not single stories but two or more tales skillfully interwoven for a total effect. If it had not been for Shakespeare breaking the classical unities, then movies, television, and the theater would be drastically different today.

Shakespeare's continuing relevance can be seen in modern productions of his

The title page from the First Folio. Shakespeare's works have become such a part of the English language that people unknowingly quote him on a daily basis.

MR. WILLIAM
SHAKESPEARES
COMEDIES,
HISTORIES, &
TRAGEDIES.

Published according to the True Originall Copies.

LONDON
Printed by Isaac Iaggard, and Ed. Blount. 1623.

plays on the stage and in the movies. *Richard III,* the play about the rise and fall of a tyrant, has been successfully acted with the performers wearing Nazi uniforms and the character of Richard III crafted to appear as a Hitler-type figure. Japanese filmmaker Akira Kurosawa has stylishly adapted both *Macbeth* and *King Lear* not only to film but to Japanese language and culture (the films are titled *Castle of the Spider's Web* and *Ran,* respectively). *Romeo and Juliet* is still as popular as it ever was and has been produced on film and on the stage many times during the twentieth century, most recently as a tale of gang warfare with a hip-hop backbeat (in effect, an update of the stage and film hit of the 1950s *West Side Story*). *Hamlet, Othello, The Merchant of Venice, The Taming of the Shrew,* and

Shakespeare probably would have found it odd that his plays are studied to this day in classrooms around the world.

The Tempest (just to name a few) have all enjoyed popularity on the stage and screen in the twentieth century. So far Ben Jonson's assertion that Shakespeare "was not of an age, but for all time" [113] has proven to be true.

If Shakespeare were alive, he would find it odd that his plays are studied as literature, especially in light of the fact that he wrote his plays for performance and not for reading on the page. His plots have had such strong influences on literature that they have become common: the comedic device of one person mistaken for another (*A Comedy of Errors*), a husband who tames his unruly wife by giving her a taste of her own medicine (*The Taming of the Shrew*), the ill-fated love of two young people from rival families (*Romeo and Juliet*), the evil king who dies as a result of his own wrongdoing and recognizes his mistake too late (*Macbeth*), and the man who is torn between loyalty and revenge (*Hamlet*). They are a few of the Shakespearean plot devices that are still in use today.

William Shakespeare has had a lasting impact not only on English literature but also on the people who create literature and other types of art. The early-twentieth-century poet T. S. Eliot refers to *Hamlet* and *The Tempest* in his famous poem "The Waste Land." The English poet John Milton was influenced by Shakespeare's righteous villains Richard III and Macbeth in describing his own righteous villain, Satan, in his long poem *Paradise Lost.* The German philosopher Friedrich Nietzsche liked to compare his idea of the "superman" to Shakespeare's *Hamlet.* The Italian composer Giuseppe Verdi, who was a lifelong fan of Shakespeare, turned three of his plays into operas. Shakespeare has not only influenced English literature and English

Shakespeare's Influence After His Death

Fourteen years after his death, William Shakespeare was still influencing English writers, a tradition that continues today. In this poem by John Milton, which prefaced the Second Folio of Shakespeare's plays, Milton responds to the complaint that Shakespeare should have been buried someplace more fabulous than Stratford (the poem is reprinted here as it appears in The Norton Anthology of English Literature*):*

"What needs my Shakespeare for his honored bones
the labor of an age in piled stones,
Or that his hallowed relics should be hid
Under a star-ypointing pyramid?
Dear son of memory, great heir of fame,
What need'st thou such weak witness of thy name?
Thou in our wonder and astonishment
Hast built thyself a livelong monument.
For whilst to th' shame of slow-endeavoring art
thy easy numbers flow, and that each heart
Hath from the leaves of thy unvalued book
Those Delphic lines with deep impression took,
Then thou, our fancy of itself bereaving,
Dost make us marble with too much conceiving;
And so sepulchered in such pomp dost lie,
that kings for such a tomb would wish to die."

authors but has also had an international influence as well, stretching beyond the realm of the printed page and into the mediums of philosophy and music.

Shakespeare has become such an integral part of English-speaking culture that it is hard to gauge his influence. He is certainly responsible for coining new words and colorful phrases that have become a common part of the English language. His plots have become such an ingrained part of entertainment that they are constantly recycled. Shakespeare has had such a huge impact on English-speaking culture that even small children will say "To be or not to be" when they are trying to be dramatic, and many know the story of *Romeo and Juliet* from cartoons. It is safe to say that if Shakespeare had never existed then our world would be drastically different from the way it is today, especially in terms of language and entertainment. It is little wonder that people refer to William Shakespeare as "The Bard" because, in a sense, he is the poet of the English language. Shakespeare the man may have died in 1616 but his spirit, and his works, are still alive and with us today. As at least one person has observed: "After God, only Shakespeare created more."[114]

Notes

Chapter 1: Shakespeare's Early Life

1. William Shakespeare, *The Tragedy of Richard III*, in *The Riverside Shakespeare*, ed. G. Blakemore Evans. Boston: Houghton Mifflin, 1974, p. 713 (I.i.54–55).

2. William Shakespeare, *The Tragedy of Romeo and Juliet*, in *The Riverside Shakespeare*, p. 1,069 (II.ii.156–57).

3. William Shakespeare, *The Taming of the Shrew*, in *The Riverside Shakespeare*, p. 127 (III.ii.150).

4. William Shakespeare, *The Second Part of Henry the Sixth*, in *The Riverside Shakespeare*, p. 658 (IV.viii.32–57).

5. Ben Jonson, "To the Memory of My Beloved, the Author, Mr. William Shakespeare, and What He Hath Left Us," in *The Norton Anthology of English Literature*, vol. 1, 6th ed., ed. M. H. Abrams. New York: Norton, 1993, p. 1,242.

6. Edmund Chambers, *A Short Life of Shakespeare with the Sources*, ed. Charles Williams. London: Oxford University Press, 1963, p. 14.

7. Quoted in S. Schoenbaum, *William Shakespeare: A Compact Documentary Life*. New York: Oxford University Press, 1987, p. 73.

8. William Shakespeare, *A Midsummer Night's Dream*, in *The Riverside Shakespeare*, p. 230 (II.ii.41–42, 56–59).

9. William Shakespeare, *The Tempest*, in *The Riverside Shakespeare*, p. 1,628 (IV.i.15–22).

Chapter 2: The Early Years in London

10. Shakespeare, *The Taming of the Shrew*, p. 117 (I.ii.50–52).

11. Quoted in Louis B. Wright, *Shakespeare's England*. New York: American Heritage, 1964, pp. 33–34.

12. Joseph Papp and Elizabeth Kirkland, *Shakespeare Alive!* New York: Bantam Books, 1988, p. 109.

13. Quoted in Papp and Kirkland, *Shakespeare Alive!* p. 112.

14. A. L. Rowse, *Shakespeare the Man*. New York: St. Martin's Press, 1988, p. 43.

15. Levi Fox, *The Shakespeare Handbook*. Boston: G. K. Hall, 1987, p. 112.

16. Thomas Nashe, "Contemporary Notices of the Plays and Poems," in *The Riverside Shakespeare*, p. 1,837.

17. Robert Greene, "Life Records and Contemporary References," in *The Riverside Shakespeare*, p. 1,835.

18. William Shakespeare, *The Third Part of Henry the Sixth*, in *The Riverside Shakespeare*, p. 677 (I.iv.137).

19. Greene, "Life Records and Contemporary References," p. 1,835.

20. Henry Chettle, "Life Records and Contemporary References," in *The Riverside Shakespeare*, p. 1,836.

21. Fox, *The Shakespeare Handbook*, p. 92.

22. Fox, *The Shakespeare Handbook*, p. 94.

23. Quoted in Schoenbaum, *William Shakespeare*, pp. 167–68.

24. Quoted in Schoenbaum, *William Shakespeare*, p. 176.

25. William Shakespeare, "Venus and Adonis," in *The Riverside Shakespeare*, p. 1,705.

26. Schoenbaum, *William Shakespeare*, pp. 174, 178.

27. Nicholas Rowe, *Some Account of the Life &c. of Mr. William Shakespear*, at *The Shakespeare Resource Page*, Http://daphne.palomar.edu/SHAKESPEARE/rowe.htm.

28. Chambers, *A Short Life of Shakespeare with the Sources*, p. 124.

Chapter 3: The Lord Chamberlain's Men

29. Anonymous, "Contemporary Notices of the Plays and Poems," in *The Riverside Shakespeare*, p. 1,838.

30. William Shakespeare, *Love's Labor's Lost,* in *The Riverside Shakespeare,* p. 179 (I.i.9–10).

31. G. Blakemore Evans, "Sir Thomas More: The Additions Ascribed to Shakespeare," in *The Riverside Shakespeare.* p. 1,684.

32. Rowse, *Shakespeare the Man,* pp. 111–12.

33. Quoted in Schoenbaum, *William Shakespeare,* p. 185.

34. Quoted in Rowse, *Shakespeare the Man,* p. 119.

35. Fox, *The Shakespeare Handbook,* p. 128.

36. William Shakespeare, *The Merchant of Venice,* in *The Riverside Shakespeare,* p. 259 (I.iii.149–51).

37. Fox, *The Shakespeare Handbook,* p. 119.

38. Quoted in Schoenbaum, *William Shakespeare,* pp. 195–96.

39. Schoenbaum, *William Shakespeare,* p. 197.

Chapter 4: First the Globe, Then the World

40. Quoted in Fox, *The Shakespeare Handbook,* p. 70.

41. Schoenbaum, *William Shakespeare,* p. 207.

42. Schoenbaum, *William Shakespeare,* p. 207.

43. Quoted in Schoenbaum, *William Shakespeare,* p. 208.

44. Rowse, *Shakespeare the Man,* pp. 144–45.

45. Quoted in Schoenbaum, *William Shakespeare,* pp. 203–204.

46. Chambers, *A Short Life of Shakespeare with the Sources,* p. 49.

47. Rowse, *Shakespeare the Man,* p. 121.

48. Fox, *The Shakespeare Handbook,* p. 123.

49. William Shakespeare, *Much Ado About Nothing,* in *The Riverside Shakespeare,* p. 336 (I.iii.13–15).

50. Shakespeare, *The Tragedy of Richard III,* p. 713 (I.i.30–31, 37).

51. Thomas Platter, "Contemporary Notices of the Plays and Poems," in *The Riverside Shakespeare,* p. 1,839.

52. William Shakespeare, *The Tragedy of Hamlet, Prince of Denmark,* in *The Riverside Shakespeare,* pp. 1,160 (III.i.55), 1,179 (V.i.184).

53. Frank Kermode, Introduction to *The Tragedy of Hamlet, Prince of Denmark,* p. 1,135.

54. Shakespeare, *The Tragedy of Hamlet, Prince of Denmark,* p. 1,185 (V.ii.380–85).

55. John Manningham, "Contemporary Notices of the Plays and Poems," in *The Riverside Shakespeare,* p. 1,840.

56. Anne Barton, Introduction to *Twelfth Night,* in *The Riverside Shakespeare,* p. 406.

57. Fox, *The Shakespeare Handbook,* pp. 146, 147.

58. Anne Barton, Introduction to *The History of Troilus and Cressida,* in *The Riverside Shakespeare,* pp. 446–47.

59. Rowse, *Shakespeare the Man,* p. 173.

60. Quoted in Rowse, *Shakespeare the Man,* p. 165.

61. Quoted in Rowse, *Shakespeare the Man,* p. 165.

62. Chambers, *A Short Life of Shakespeare with the Sources,* p. 45.

63. Schoenbaum, *William Shakespeare,* p. 232.

64. Quoted in Schoenbaum, *William Shakespeare,* p. 249.

Chapter 5: The King's Men

65. Schoenbaum, *William Shakespeare,* pp. 249–50.

66. Quoted in "Documents Relating to the Theatre," in *The Riverside Shakespeare,* p. 1,851.

67. Papp and Kirkland, *Shakespeare Alive!* p. 123.

68. Fox, *The Shakespeare Handbook,* p. 157.

69. Fox, *The Shakespeare Handbook,* p. 156.

70. Peter Levi, *The Life and Times of William Shakespeare.* New York: Henry Holt, 1988, p. 269.

71. Fox, *The Shakespeare Handbook,* p. 163.

72. Fox, *The Shakespeare Handbook,* p. 163.

73. Levi, *The Life and Times of William Shakespeare,* p. 258.

74. Rowse, *Shakespeare the Man,* p. 190.

75. Levi, *The Life and Times of William Shakespeare,* p. 256.

76. William Shakespeare, *The Tragedy of Macbeth,* in *The Riverside Shakespeare,* pp. 1,379 (IV.i.80–81), 1,339 (V.viii.15–16).

77. Shakespeare, *The Tragedy of Macbeth*, p. 1,330 (IV.i.117).

78. Levi, *The Life and Times of William Shakespeare*, pp. 277–78.

79. Rowse, *Shakespeare the Man*, pp. 184–85.

80. Quoted in Philip K. Bock, *Shakespeare and Elizabethan Culture*. New York: Schocken Books, 1984, p. 77.

81. Rowse, *Shakespeare the Man*, p. 185.

82. Rowse, *Shakespeare the Man*, pp. 198, 199.

83. Frank Kermode, Introduction to *The Life of Timon of Athens*, in *The Riverside Shakespeare*, p. 1,443.

84. Fox, *The Shakespeare Handbook*, p. 166.

85. Quoted in Hallett Smith, Introduction to *Pericles, Prince of Tyre*, in *The Riverside Shakespeare*, p. 1,482.

86. Fox, *The Shakespeare Handbook*, p. 170.

Chapter 6: Back to Stratford

87. Quoted in Schoenbaum, *William Shakespeare*, p. 279.

88. Fox, *The Shakespeare Handbook*, p. 49.

89. Schoenbaum, *William Shakespeare*, p. 272.

90. Quoted in Schoenbaum, *William Shakespeare*, p. 272.

91. Sir Henry Wotton, "Contemporary Notices of the Plays and Poems," in *The Riverside Shakespeare*, pp. 1,842–843.

92. Hallett Smith, Introduction to *The Winter's Tale*, in *The Riverside Shakespeare*, pp. 1,567, 1,568.

93. Greene, "Life Records and Contemporary References," p. 1,835.

94. William Shakespeare, *The Tempest*, in *The Riverside Shakespeare*, p. 1,617 (I.ii.402).

95. Hallett Smith, Introduction to *The Tempest*, p. 1,606.

96. Shakespeare, *The Tempest*, p. 1,630 (IV.i.147–58).

97. Shakespeare, *The Tempest*, p. 1,632 (V.i.48–57).

98. Quoted in Smith, Introduction to *The Tempest*, p. 1,610.

99. Fox, *The Shakespeare Handbook*, p. 125.

100. Schoenbaum, *William Shakespeare*, p. 293.

101. Quoted in Schoenbaum, *William Shakespeare*, p. 293.

102. Quoted in Schoenbaum, *William Shakespeare*, p. 296.

103. Quoted in Schoenbaum, *William Shakespeare*, pp. 295–96.

104. Quoted in Schoenbaum, *William Shakespeare*, p. 298.

105. William Shakespeare, "Shakespeare's Will," in *The Riverside Shakespeare*, p. 1,833.

106. Shakespeare, "Shakespeare's Will," p. 1,833.

107. Schoenbaum, *William Shakespeare*, p. 302.

108. William Shakespeare, "Life Records and Contemporary References," in *The Riverside Shakespeare*, p. 1,834.

109. Unknown, "Life Records and Contemporary References," in *The Riverside Shakespeare*, p. 1,834.

Chapter 7: Shakespeare Today

110. Henry Condell and John Heminge, "Contemporary Allusions (to the First Folio, 1623)," in Chambers, *A Short Life of Shakespeare with the Sources*, p. 220.

111. Papp and Kirkland, *Shakespeare Alive!* p. 123.

112. Fox, *The Shakespeare Handbook*, p. 174.

113. Jonson, "To the Memory of My Beloved, the Author, Mr. William Shakespeare, and What He Hath Left Us," p. 1,242 (43).

114. James Joyce, citing Alexandre Dumas, *Ulysses*.

Chronology of Shakespeare's Works

1589–1590	*Henry VI Part 1*	1599	*Henry V*
1590–1591	*Henry VI Part 2*	1599	*Julius Caesar*
1590–1591	*Henry VI Part 3*	1599	*As You Like It*
1590–1593	*Sir Thomas More*	1600–1601	*Hamlet*
1592–1593	*Richard III*	1601	"The Phoenix and the Turtle"
1592–1593	*The Comedy of Errors*	1601	*Twelfth Night*
1592–1593	"Venus and Adonis"	1601–1602	*Troilus and Cressida*
1593–1594	*Titus Andronicus*	1602–1603	*All's Well That Ends Well*
1593–1594	"The Rape of Lucrece"	1604	*Measure for Measure*
1593–1594	*The Taming of the Shrew*	1604	*Othello*
1593–1595	*Sonnets*	1605	*King Lear*
1594	*The Two Gentlemen of Verona*	1606	*Macbeth*
1594–1595	*Love's Labor's Lost*	1606	*Antony and Cleopatra*
1594–1595	*King John*	1607–1608	*Coriolanus*
1595	*Richard II*	1607–1608	*Timon of Athens*
1595–1596	*Romeo and Juliet*	1607–1608	*Pericles*
1595–1596	*A Midsummer Night's Dream*	1609–1610	*Cymbeline*
1596–1597	*The Merchant of Venice*	1610–1611	*The Winter's Tale*
1596–1597	*Henry IV Part 1*	1611	*The Tempest*
1597	*The Merry Wives of Windsor*	1612	*Henry VIII*
1598	*Henry IV Part 2*	1612–1613	*Cardenio*
1598–1599	*Much Ado About Nothing*	1613	*The Two Noble Kinsmen*

For Further Reading

Ivor Brown, *Shakespeare in His Time*. Edinburgh: Nelson, 1960. Although somewhat dated, this book is still considered one of the classics of Shakespeare scholarship. It examines the society Shakespeare lived in and the historical events he lived through. This book is recommended for serious Shakespeare scholars.

S. H. Burton, *Shakespeare's Life and Stage*. Edinburgh: Chambers, 1989. A recent, and comprehensive, account of Shakespeare's life both on and off the stage. The language in places can be intimidating, but for the reader with patience, and a dictionary, it can be very rewarding.

Victor Cahn, *Shakespeare the Playwright*. New York: Greenwood Press, 1991. This book is both easy to read and engrossing. It examines the plays Shakespeare produced and offers some interesting speculation on what inspired him. It is highly recommended because it is well researched and well written.

Richard Dutton, *William Shakespeare: A Literary Life*. New York: St. Martin's Press, 1989. This is an unusual biography of Shakespeare because its focus is limited to his production as a playwright and the probable literary sources that influenced him. This book is recommended for the serious researcher.

E. A. J. Honigmann, *Shakespeare's Impact on His Contemporaries*. London: Macmillan Press, 1982. An interesting book that examines Shakespeare's influence on his fellow writers. It is well researched, well written, and a valuable tool for evaluating Shakespeare's importance in his own age. Recommended for the confident reader with a general interest.

Dennis Kay, *Shakespeare: His Life, Work, and Era*. New York: Morrow, 1992. This is an ambitious book that attempts to examine all aspects of Shakespeare's world. Although it contains many interesting details, the average reader may find it tedious to read. Recommended for researchers.

W. Nicholas Knight, *Shakespeare's Hidden Life: Shakespeare at the Law 1585–1595*. New York: Mason and Lipscomb, 1973. This is a good book to read to get an idea about the controversy surrounding how Shakespeare spent the Lost Years. Knight's idea that Shakespeare spent the Lost Years as a lawyer's assistant is largely ignored today.

Gary O'Connor, *William Shakespeare: A Life*. London: Hodder and Stoughton, 1991. This biography of Shakespeare is geared toward the general reader. The examination of Shakespeare's life is standard and offers no new insights. Contains illustrations.

A. L. Rowse, *Shakespeare the Elizabethan*. New York: Putnam Books, 1977. Rowse is a good writer, and this is an excellent examination of Shakespeare as a product of Elizabethan England. Although Rowse does have a tendency to fictionalize, his books still have scholastic merit. Recommended for all readers. Contains pictures.

Eric Sams, *The Real Shakespeare*. New Haven, CT: Yale University Press, 1995. A recent biography that purports to examine the life of the "real" Shakespeare. Although it is a bit sensationalistic, it does contain some interesting ideas about Shakespeare.

Peter Thomson, *Shakespeare's Professional Career*. Cambridge: Cambridge University Press, 1992. This book examines Shakespeare as a professional playwright and theater man. It is well written and well researched and tends to portray Shakespeare as a shrewd businessman. Recommended to anyone with an interest in Shakespeare.

Stanley Wells, *Shakespeare: A Dramatic Life*. London: Sinclair-Stevenson, 1994. This analysis of Shakespeare's life as a professional in the theaters of the Renaissance is well presented. The language is clear and ideas are presented in a systematic fashion. Contains a few illustrations.

Stanley Wells, *Shakespeare the Writer and His Work*. New York: Scribner and Sons, 1978. This book examines Shakespeare's creative side and how it developed throughout his life. It can be rather dense in places, but it is recommended for anyone with an interest in Shakespeare.

Works Consulted

M. H. Abrams, ed., *The Norton Anthology of English Literature*. Vol. 1, 6th ed. New York: Norton, 1993. A college-level anthology that covers English literature from the Middle Ages through the Renaissance and to the eighteenth century. Useful for studying Shakespeare for the background material it contains on the Renaissance and because it provides quick reference to Shakespeare's contemporaries and their works. Contains glossary, footnotes, and index.

Philip K. Bock, *Shakespeare and Elizabethan Culture*. New York: Schocken Books, 1984. An ambitious and learned book that examines Elizabethan society through the lens of anthropology and as portrayed in Shakespeare's works. Despite its academic tone, it is surprisingly easy to read, and although it provides little biographical information on Shakespeare, it is useful for gaining an idea of the type of society Shakespeare lived in.

Edmund Chambers, *A Short Life of Shakespeare with the Sources*. Ed. Charles Williams. London: Oxford University Press, 1963. This book is an abridgement of Chambers's two-volume *William Shakespeare: A Study of Facts and Problems*. Chambers's original book is still considered to be the authoritative study of Shakespeare's life even though it was printed in 1930. This shortened version of Chambers's longer work still retains the documents and observations that made Chambers famous but omits the Latin and legal phrases that made the original work hard to read and understand. Chambers is an excellent scholar and not only provides the facts of Shakespeare's life but examines the many legends surrounding his existence. The primary value of this book is that it provides copies of documents and commentaries on Shakespeare's life in an easy-to-handle format.

Maurice Charney, *All of Shakespeare*. New York: Columbia University Press, 1993. An excellent book that explains in simple language Shakespeare's plays and poems. It is very useful for clarifying obscure parts of his works. Recommended for the student having trouble understanding Shakespeare.

Mark Eccles, *Shakespeare in Warwickshire*. Madison: Wisconsin University Press, 1961. A landmark study of the social history of Stratford-upon-Avon. It also spells out what is known of Shakespeare's friends, neighbors, and ancestors. The language of this book is somewhat dense and is meant for the Shakespeare specialist.

G. Blakemore Evans, ed., *The Riverside Shakespeare*. Boston: Houghton Mifflin, 1974. The subtitle of this book should be "All you wanted to know about Shakespeare and were afraid to ask." At two and a half inches thick and with 1,927 pages, it has everything: all the plays, all the poems, copies of documents Shakespeare signed, copies of commentaries on Shakespeare from the Renaissance, explanatory essays by modern critics on each of the plays, a biography, a history of English drama, a glossary, footnotes, plenty of pictures, and more. The best thing about *The Riverside Shakespeare* is that it is rather easy to read and understand. Recommended for anyone with an interest in Shakespeare.

Levi Fox, *The Shakespeare Handbook.* Boston: G. K. Hall, 1987. An excellent source for all types of information on Shakespeare. Contains a brief biography, a history of English drama during the reigns of Queen Elizabeth and King James, summarizations of the plays, discussions on the music and songs of Shakespeare, and more. Easy to read with lots of full-color pictures, this book is recommended for all ages and all reading levels.

Russell Fraser, *Young Shakespeare.* New York: Columbia University Press, 1988. A scholarly and exhaustive study of Shakespeare's youth in Stratford and London. It provides interesting insights into Shakespeare's marriage, his family life, and the probable motive for him leaving Stratford for London. Although it contains valuable information, the language in places is very dense. This book is meant for the serious Shakespeare scholar.

Norman Holland, ed., *Shakespeare's Personality.* Berkeley and Los Angeles: University of California Press, 1989. A collection of essays by various modern critics that examines elements of Shakespeare's psyche and life. Little biographical information. The essays range from the easily read and understood to the obscure. Meant for English undergraduate students and Shakespeare scholars.

Peter Levi, *The Life and Times of William Shakespeare.* New York: Henry Holt, 1988. A mediocre biography of Shakespeare that draws much of its biographical material from what Shakespeare wrote. More speculation than fact, it tends to romanticize Shakespeare, but not as badly as other writers have. It is an easy and informative book to read. Few illustrations.

Joseph Papp and Elizabeth Kirkland, *Shakespeare Alive!* New York: Bantam Books, 1988. An excellent book that explores the society of Elizabethan England. It provides information on Elizabethan superstitions, family life, theaters, the staging of plays, and the status of women, among other things. It is an interesting book and is easy to read. Although it does not cover Shakespeare's life, this book does provide insights into what Shakespeare's life must have been like. Few pictures and no index.

A. L. Rowse, *Shakespeare the Man.* New York: St. Martin's Press, 1988. A rather fanciful biography of Shakespeare that tends more toward romantic speculation than to actual facts. Despite its faults, it is still informative and easy to read. Rowse's thoughts on the "Dark Lady" of the sonnets are especially interesting. The book is well documented and contains many facts, but Rowse tends to romanticize Shakespeare into a larger-than-life figure. This book is recommended for readers of all ages who have an interest in the life of Shakespeare. Contains few pictures and an index.

S. Schoenbaum, *Shakespeare's Lives.* New York: Oxford University Press, 1970.

Comprehensive biography of Shakespeare covering the facts of his actual life. It also records the legends associated with Shakespeare and weighs their validity. Recommended for the serious Shakespeare scholar.

—————, *Shakespeare: The Globe and the World.* New York: Oxford University Press, 1979. Basically an illustrated catalog of the manuscripts, books, and art objects that belong to the Folger Shakespeare Library in Washington, D.C. It also contains a text by Schoenbaum that discusses Shakespeare's life in relation to the pictured objects. It is an excellent source for information on Shakespeare and the society in which he lived.

—————, *William Shakespeare: A Compact Documentary Life.* New York: Oxford University Press, 1987. Basically a combination of the other three books plus a fourth (*William Shakespeare: A Documentary Life*). Contains few illustrations but does contain all the relevant facts and speculations on Shakespeare's life in an easy-to-handle (as compared to the two-volume *Documentary Life*) and easy-to-read format. Recommended for anyone with an interest in Shakespeare. Schoenbaum is this author's favorite Shakespeare scholar because his writing is clear, the book is well organized, and he sticks to the facts and does not romanticize the man.

—————, *William Shakespeare: Records and Images.* New York: Oxford University Press, 1981. Contains photographs and reproductions of various documents relating to the life of Shakespeare along with explanatory notes. Comprehensive and scholarly, this book is meant for the serious Shakespeare scholar.

Joseph Sobran, *Alias Shakespeare.* New York: Free Press, 1997. The most recent attempt at debunking the notion that William Shakespeare wrote the plays and poems attributed to him. Sobran argues that Edward de Vere, earl of Oxford, was the actual author of the plays and poems. Although Sobran argues his points convincingly, he tends to ignore facts that are accepted by the majority of Shakespearean scholars, and as a result the book is one-sided. This book is recommended for those who are curious about the argument against Shakespeare's authorship and want to learn about the reasoning behind the assertion.

Diane Stanley and Peter Vennema, *Bard of Avon: The Story of William Shakespeare.* New York: Morrow Junior Books, 1992. An excellent, award-winning biography of Shakespeare written for young readers. It contains accurate information and is beautifully illustrated. This book is highly recommended for children of all ages.

E. M. W. Tillyard, *The Elizabethan World Picture.* New York: Vintage Books, ca. 1941. A brief and illuminating account of the ideas of world order prevalent in the Elizabethan age. Discusses the Renaissance ideas of the Chain of Being, the Four Humours, the Four Elements, and others. Easy to read and easy to understand. A must for anyone wanting to learn about the Elizabethan mind-set.

Louis B. Wright, *Shakespeare's England.* New York: American Heritage, 1964. A lavishly illustrated biography of Shakespeare set against the background of Renaissance England. Not only does it provide information on Shakespeare's life but it provides brief biographies of people who had an effect on Shakespeare. The book does a great job of combining biographical information with historical events to give a full picture of Shakespeare and the society in which he lived. Recommended for anyone with an interest in Shakespeare.

Internet Sources

The Complete Works of William Shakespeare. Http://the-tech.mit.edu/Shakespeare/works   This website provides not only the complete works of Shakespeare, which can be downloaded, but also a concordance that allows for searching the works for specific words or phrases. Also contains a brief biography of Shakespeare along with an electronic version of *Bartlett's Familiar Quotations.* It is an invaluable source of information for the student researching Shakespeare.

(No Title). Http://www.springfield.k12.il.us/schools/springfield/eliz/everylife.html   Although it is written and maintained by high school students in Springfield, Illinois, this site contains articles on a variety of Elizabethan institutions. It is easy to use, well thought out, and very informative. Subjects range from crime and punishment to medical practices.

The Shakespeare Resource Page. Http://daphne.palomar.edu/SHAKESPEARE/   Contains an annotated guide to the scholarly resources available on the Internet. It also presents research material that is unavailable elsewhere such as a complete copy of Nicholas Rowe's *Some Account of the Life &c. of Mr. William Shakespear.*

Shakey's Place. Http://library. advanced.org/10502/entry.html   A good site that contains the text of the plays and poems along with artwork inspired by Shakespeare.

Index

Picture Credits

About the Author

Thomas Thrasher received his master of fine arts degree from California State University, Long Beach. He has written two books of poetry and has published poems in magazines across the country. He currently lives in Southern California with his cat Jinx and goes surfing whenever he can.